The Pilgrimage

The Pilgrimage

Selected Poems: 1962-2012

Dave Oliphant

LAMAR UNIVERSITY press

ISBN: 978-0-9852552-4-4
Library of Congress Control Number: 2012953845

Book Design: Elizabeth R. Charles
Manufactured in the United States of America

Lamar University Press
Beaumont, Texas

Acknowledgments

I am grateful to Road Runner Press, Prickly Pear Press, Thorp Springs Press, Host Publications, and Wings Press for publishing my books.

The poems in this collection previously appeared in the following publications:

doubt & REDOUTE, 1962
Once and 6 Others, 1966
Brands, 1972
Taking Stock, 1973
Lines & Mounds, 1976
Footprints, 1961-1978, 1978
Austin, 1985
María's Poems, 1987
Memories of Texas Towns & Cities, 2000
Backtracking, 2004
KD a Jazz Biography, 2012

Some of these poems originally appeared in *Aileron, Cedar Rock, Chawed Rawzin, College English, The Colorado Quarterly, Cream City Review, descant, From Hide and Horn* (Eakin Press), *Fuse, Illinois Quarterly, Lucille, New Letters, New Texas '95, Nimrod, Pax, Sarcophagus, Seems, Sleepy Tree Book II, South Dakota Review, Southern Poetry Review, The Texas Observer, Texas Short Stories & Poems* (Texas Center for Writers Press), and *Thicket*.

to my beauty
María Isabel Jofré Aguirre

Contents

Order of Worship

Rooming this Austin autumn
up over a couple it sounds
like to me is just about to
come apart at the seams,

I shut out the matter of
presumptuous me, set the
round black primer down
onto this turning table,

offer a prayer that im-
mortal air bless with a
loan of all twelve tones
brain ear lung & active liver.

Amplifier on, hear below!
Stretch your every lobe
unto this flowering platter.
Palms to breast & chest of

drawers, feel where, deep
in bones & boards, psalm-
like vibrates his 1st sonata,
Masselos at the piano.

Of the morrow's rent,
of the neighbor's knock,
take never a note, guaran-
teed the underwear's sewn

with more than patches
from quaint hymn tunes,
when the pastor-insurer's
America's revivaled reliever,

music's old line legal
investor-singer of spiritual
vernacular to heartache & fever:
Charles E. Ives, reweaver!

The Sky Begins to Smolder

  white fluffy ash
  covering fast
  sticking to the stones
  lining naked limbs

the words begin to drift:

  soft embossed thoughts
  coming slowly
  to stay and feed the cold and
  barren day, dress
  the shivering heart

halfway through it stops
the dripping drops win out:

  but not within
  for the fire is free
  winter has no hold
  the clouds contained a spark

The Porter's Resurrection

as last night's gar
        ascends to form a fume
cigar ash drifts down
             to meet his broom
       (the fish now floating
           in a breath of smoke)

between this passage—up &
                   down—
       of death
there's little left
       but the scratching of his sweep
and the thought of tomorrow's
       late-Sunday-morning sleep

Cotton Payday

a pale picker
on padded knees
spurns the sand
that burns between his toes
as he plucks green bolls
from acrid shrubs
and on the sly
drops a rock into
his trailing sack
weighs his load
on scales of justice
his pay is born
of trust

while whirling winds
gather dust
to hurl in heavy eyes
a black of the earth
working two rows at once
quickly bares
the clothing trees
stuffing white clouds into
the only wedding train
she'll ever wear

at week's end
she heads on home
on thankful feet
for hand-me-downs
her leaning shack
her lazy garden patch
as the pale one lightly trips
around the town
and finds a movie house

In Memory of Wallace Stevens

Early in the day
the bloom to her face
has faded away.
On this dry-run map
withered leaves now trace
to a stream's cracked bed
yearnings of her sap.
One silken tent, spread
within her bosom,
catches the dew from
                    each
night's cooling cry.
Her sweet cypress knees
pious dogs now fry
                    and,
canine burnt, hymns
are turning to pleas
heaven politely
                hears.
        No dog star harms,
but cowbirds tritely
bend her tender limbs,
robbing fruitless charms.

O redbird on the roof,
a "torrent will fall"
on this dying church
when
            flying from your
                    gabled perch
you nest and sing
            a blue-green proof
that earth and sky are all.

Revelation

Flying against plate glass
the moonlit owl
finds himself facing a prey
he's cracked
but cannot penetrate.

Such a web obscures the view
as does a breath of hate
passing blindly through
a thrown rock's hole
to howl endlessly
night and day.

2

On an afternoon
warm though autumn
the water was calm,
the tree so still.

Of a sudden the wind arose,
parting clouds,
casting on the mirror
a bird's crushed unknowing face.

Afterwards the bright red sun went out
and the clumsy gale lay down.

The tree stood
overtaken by the lake
. . . a club-footed boat
brushed the top-most branch,

slowly trolling above the garden,
between dark and the broken deep.

Once

in trekking trails
littered with the bones
of love, he saw himself

as a swarm of bees,
each dream con-
ceiving from the

brightest of weeds
honey in the carcass
of a mountain sheep,

white or plain un-
painted hive,
what nation

mattered not,
while in between the
visions, how seldom

fair history admits
in those torrid,
forward times, of

prairie schooners,
not all rolled
East to West,

explorers, at first,
so full of goal,
retraced courageous steps,

weighing anchors, setting sails,
as on the side
Fats Waller sang,

played it all in fun:
"Wull looka there,
Christie's grabbed

the Sainta Marie
and he's goin' back!"
blacks in earnest

shipping to Liberia,
Siberia of the U.S.A.?
or then too

a Toby in print, quitting
the Typees, a gentle
Núñez, his medicine

needed, writing
Naufragios instead,
can't do both, so drama:

"a wave caught us . . .
heaved the barge
a horse-shoe throw"—

sure sign of a lucky land!
Cabeza de Vaca & his men
safely on Galveston isle,

living, as its natives did,
off locust beans, pecans & such,
unfortunate only in this:

escaping THE TOWN OF HEARTS,
found soon enough "an Indian
wearing around his neck

a little sword-belt buckle

with a horse-shoe nail
stitched to it"—a trinket

no more, harmless it seemed,
but then, with tribes extinct
(the last Karankaway

putting out to sea), proved,
or so it was felt to be, a curse,
tied, to the Spanish tongue –

& thus another
"poet of desolation,"
cold at dawn,

warming later on,
settles there
on her petal's edge,

alights barely, only to fly,
a morning dew,
making, like all the

rest, a beeline back,
as if, which it was,
the very sun

those too once wearied of,
despairing, rather,
he'd drink too deep,

burn her tender blades,
dull them to
his freckled face,

with wooden thoughts,
his unfocused words
wagons out of control,

caught as if in a
blue-white blur,
till wheels & dreams

seemed western-like,
an RKO production,
an overland stage,

its spokes
turning in sun,
backwards to the coach's course,

as by their opening,
closing view, the
wandering, would-be pioneers

grew bewildered too,
wondering each day
where better lay:

ahead
thru a
green

gulf of flowering marijuana
or hitched yet
to a tobacco past,

while he would go
with enemies of the Conquistador,
los Araucanos, though even those,

so bellicose, "left almost no
meaningful relics" –
in Arica, abandoned claims

he'd stake, of artifacts,
a few up north,

dumb survivors

of Incan rites—
inundated by immigration,
a flood

freed the land,
freed it for
the European—

& at the feet
of her savage hills
Chile's hopes

then writ large,
on rocks,
in letters

blue with red:
Allende, Alessandri, Frei,
políticos,

silt settled
in a continental-
indian blend,

a country-wide con-
coction,
admixture it seemed

with the wind, of blood's
dark
& skin's white wine,

in song celebrated long,
at the end of the soccer,
the COPPER-built field,

where the goalie
stands alone:
the one sound,

the other strong,
how bring them together
in the awkward lines of a

poem? enters here a shopper,
wondering perhaps
if he might have

something in the way of . . .
love, skiing off-key
down Andean slopes of

snow,
sprawling as Santiago,
soldiers, amputees,

feeling their toes
still there, his fin-
gers her hair,

itching emptily,
with sycamore stumps
leafless then on

Bernardo O'Higgins Boulevard:
footprints, images to follow,
dissonant tones to re-

solve, a
practice
seasonal

in a tract reaches
from desert sand to polar ice

(though a hint hardly

taken, ever at war
with himself, asks
rather, what good would it

do? too soon traps his
animal sense): —Chile,
skinny & at the sea, out of it

the delicacies,
locos dipped *en limón*,
tidal waves in turn

exacting pay, tremblings known
as *sismos*–earthquakes,
but these in his mind:

forest / plain
farm / city
remorse / reverie—

the crust
moving,
cracking the

walls, whereon
poverty
paints, writes its

bold white cries for the
SOIL: death or the
Rio Maipo–his daily prayer

that, as that river,
ink ever flow, such lifeblood
come from a pen,

that song
link lands
& lingos,

but the cost
in dollars &
cents,

his flimsy excuse,
then, too,
stimulus

for swimming,
mounting,
time & again–once

it might be done,
o tormenta,
what need in another rise,

a bathing beach
breakers create, his thoughts
then fashioning one

where boulders were before,
another walk along it,
but without any squaw,

emotion awash,
pack rats of storms
would strand him there,

penguin-like,
on her Viña shore,
only to have

his honied flight,
his faithful eyes

sucked, plucked

by an undertow, his ears,
like shells, ringing with a foreign,
a wordless echoing

carried upon the air, here
where, though all things
seem secure,

he feels no fool
straining far
still to recall the

lamb's ascent
on pollened wings,
up from the fields

of yellow wildflowers,
told him then
by an Indian name,

though seen as leaves
dusty in the sun,
just weeds—reckoned

for another race,
forgotten by all
but industries

of sign-
posts & potteries,
yet growing too

in memories of
those northern roads, of the
eucalyptus leaf,

which silvers first,
reddens then,
yet ends up green,

& these he knew as the
ages of men, but ages
reversed by love . . . of a

sudden, a burst from the
crowd: how, in the arms
of a puny guard? look

to what language for
answer? —epileptic
seen in the mines:

becomes him then, jerks,
raves that "no form of life
except the erratic penguin

has ever attained to aerial
status and later returned
to the sorry business

of plodding, paddling,
rolling, or
sliding" – finds himself

out of the game,
stretched in a clumsy em-
brace at the goal he's

missed, of the golden comb,
of the land lost,
his opposing side,

his buzzing throng within,
brought to its feet

with a cheer

for where & how he is,
happy he can't be
there,

ever applying
a salesman's
tone,

any change of mind
its con-
stant fear,

until he hears,
feels,
records a

crag against it,
another to be
scaled in

time, raising,
in residue,
a music of shards,

softly,
& for this, then,
ever,

chronicler
through the
darkest of chords.

Can a Poet Turn Gunslinger & Find Happiness?

after a cartoon by Pat Oliphant of the Denver Post

Any 3rd grader with his thinking cap on
knows pistol & poetry don't go together.

But then there's Ed Dorn's "Gunslinger,"
where his philosophical horse figures in,
an existential kind of *equus*,
though that's a gimmick,
a mincing of words,
a shooting them up
as the comic does,
like Ed Muskie's hat,
his fingers stuck through holes
"Mean Gene" McCarthy's filled
his Lincoln stovepipe with,
leaning here at the western bar
all in black,
three 45s & a short machete.

The question is
can the poet find happiness
as a college professor?

And if he were to
what would it be worth
in terms of verse?

The poet gone revolutionary,
as have so many in Chile,
has he found a trigger the cleaner release,
quicker than even a rhythmic line,
closer to the mark than rhyme?

When the Texas Rangers acquired the Colt,
was their happiness at last complete,
as they picked off the raiding Comanche,
& chased Mexicans off their stolen land?

Can we as gunmen bring the peace?
The answer is yes,
if what we go by
is a State of the Union speech.

Yet maybe Mayakovsky did indeed.
Rimbaud in Africa running arms & ammunition.
Jacques Vaché, patron saint of the Surrealists,
in the theatre & in the street,
with revolver in hand, opening up at random.

What more could they do,
once their loaded words
misfired in our pacified minds.

Brands

from comic to tragic
the Indian's design
just a man-sign

yet taken from the child
like his land
to make a cattle brand

his basic writing style
not letters or numbers
but just stick figures

some potbellied
others at prayer
a few with an extra pair

of legs or with feathers
& for white ownership
hand on hip

akimbo
a posture unknown
to the braves shown

with arms dangling
unhaughtily down
saved by the Church

enslaved by the Crown

6666

tire tracks in snow
like those the TV ads immortalize, maybe
but these carried really live
a language of the range

where seared flesh told
of men & 5 card draw

stud instead of traffic sludge
no clean hoof-printed mud but
trudging in freezing weather
to the Barb City Travel Agency
to book passage on a freighter
to & through the Panama Canal

for getting closer to where
Cortés landed his cows
no living on bread alone, no sirree
marking his meat & milk sources with

three crosses †††† black in their hides

a holy trinity / thieves at his side

DeKalb, Illinois: home of the
wire that won the West
Glidden: inventor of that industry
his family raising flowers now
doing penance perhaps by running a nursery
arranging sprays & valentines

no droppings down these streets
just another connection
but any makes the day
in that one they fenced them in
burnt them with a four sixes
red-hot white-hot iron:

tool that told as it smoked
of cigar fumes thick as fog
the dealing slow
no tricks or banded sleeves

mer taking two
ranger one

e eyes of the first suddenly lit
ad hit his pair & paired his ace
full house: enough to stake a spread
recover all he'd lost / thinking the other
must have drawn to a straight / at most a flush
calling with a ranch & a hundred head

gambling away
the dry wind-blown gulch
the sandy land where he made it a go
the newcomer naming his win
for the hand that settled him down
to a wife & seven kids

a night the herd brings back
in the blaze of day
to every prairie grazed
every shrub rubbed up against
his four of a kind written third-degree
his poker face beats prime time

H.E.L.L.

a baptism by fire
the smoking letters 16" high
the steer it's said
let out no cry

but the cow would bawl
& the calf bleat pitiably
more sensitive to the word
was spelled in him literally

so that seen for half-a-mile
that mythic sea of flame
could be read by wranglers
as a harmless rancher's name

initialed near San Antone to grow with ribs
a scar tissue hieroglyph
a practice old & indelible
as that known well by the Pharoah's Nile

but now is gone
with the cowhand's songs of the broken-

hearted brand ♡♡   a belief in what his

h e double *l* says

gone with the glad gatherings
at round-up time
with cutting out & returning of strays
though still we carry through

with its meaning in hearts
that break all singing
in meetings called to end all trust
in motel beds with pickups

black as sins you lie heavy upon that home
where merely the quote has scarred for life
with brands for slaves knifed in your name
o the cities sacked to bring your easy reign
yet how many maimed by words you never
have looked inside & found like a Jeremiah

& who says on stock your shape won't keep
their horse or beeves from a hole or disease

XIT

— BQ,
short for Barbecue Campbell,
first manager of the XIT
(10 counties in Texas,
really covered just 9),

one time newspaper man
from Batavia, Illinois,
more recently home of Dan Issel,
best basketball center I ever saw,

but the question comes:
could such a fiery scepter
have cooked the rivers & streams,
boiled the fish with potassium waste?

Central heating I'm not complaining, much,
& hot house plants you're maybe sweeter than not.
But o that open-air smell is a memory strong
as any faith I've read in a book,

& I want to breathe those bygone days,
& I want to believe in Batavia boys,
though the sulphate's got in my gills
& the buzzers keep sounding a loss.

El Afilador

blows that Indian whistle
while pushing his shop
from street to street

all now shaded by cottonwoods
with leaves I liken to arrowheads
green hearts, what have you

the tree that followed sharply upon
flowering in the face of my own
& this of dull winter's wit

as on it he announces
with special interval & scale
he's come to grind

carving knives
scissors or
what you have

I've this edge of the mind
beyond his wheel's repair
yet listen intent on the Indian tune

& find it keen
feel it fresh & clean
paring away this cheesy rind

Prehistoric Pastoral

Coming into town, Hobbs, New Mexico,
from any number of freezing spots
just north or east of here,

icicles hanging like walrus' tusks
stained bloody by a spattering of mud,
encrusted cars pass right on through

just after a café coffee break,
a tank full of sabertooth,
or four bucks of the dinosaur

at the last station open on leaving out,
where at the bell the attendant limps
to the electric window lowered a crack

to hear the driver's "Filler with reg'lar
and check them tars tuh twunty-nine."
And ever jealous of the way they'd go,

I'd feel a stranded sperm whale
cast up out of a deep I'd known,
to waste here on these hostile shores.

Bitter as the cold they travel from,
that's the way I first drove in,
having to take the one job left,

teacher in a two-bit oil town
eons behind the times,
the dog next door racing up and down,

digging a hole under *our* white fence,
crawling through, getting the puppy
to jumping, dragging linen off the line,

and that's the way we neighbors met.
Parked awhile in this kind of weather,
snow and ice soon fall right off the bumpers.

Animals' instincts snared me down a cave,
and in shame I looked for candles to trim,
trinkets of myself for common trade,

found light in exchange for blubber.

Ornette in Rome

1

Following cold months in NYC
      jobless with
love what comes in what goes out having hit

      an all-time low he prospects here
ruins rich enough to buy not
      oblivion but what

through others' weathered maps restores
      if not the golden melody: for that's
a thing of a

      foreign past   :the country touch
the tortuous trail the lost black mine
      of laugh & cry

2

same as peace tracked down to violent death
      a cooling drink to desert sand
      wholeness is now traced here
      to a back-broken land

      of torsos & shards
      years aqueducts dry
      trees tombs filled still
with triumphs long unknown yet memorized

3

patched up
      composed
            for string quartet

proved   once & for all   nobody
        like this one-man band
            could grow up   to run for & win
the Presidency   & just before in-
        auguration   the whole blamed
                blessed nation   glued to
midas TVs   celebrities
        standing out   in January snow
                poets   their laureate lines ready
tributes to   the All-American way he rose
        from rhythm & blues to the Big Chair
            where   the buck stops here
how he   (heroically)   suffered through
        in New Orleans   when honkies broke
            that white plastic sax 'cross his back
& just when   unmagic words   'bout to
        solemnize the almightiest show
            would whip   his bent trumpet
from his vaudeville tux   & trade it all
        for a couple of   electrically-rapid blasts
            illogical jewels would warm
turn the town to a jillion tears
        & weeping a belly laugh   swear that
            sorry boys & girls   I love you all
but have it   kit & caboodle   cause
        there's somewhere   in this here horn
            a bigger
richer land
        to look
                after

Breather

Carried easily to an end of August,
with Johnson grass beginning to bleed,
they pass me riding bareback, hair flying,

bare feet slapping their mares' shining sides,
trotting along in solid red shorts,
in men's loud, matching plaid sport shirts,

till reining up for resting their mounts,
in turn moving ahead, I too at a distance
take time out to catch me a breath, kneel,

and leaning backwards, put off the pack,
stand up bending this way and that, mostly
to their talk brought near on the breeze

now lifting snatches, now letting go what I've
taken to be more chompings at bits at this pair's
bridal paths, watch, hear with each horse's

shake of a head, snortings for joy under burdens,
I'd hope, neither had ever to be broken to bear,
then stretching myself in the dry grass again,

shoulder and poke each arm through its strap,
start up with a jerk, and, feeling the load lighter,
hike on in the odor of autumn in the air.

Crawling Geese on the Texas Coast

In whatever town I've found myself,
dreaming on cities free of fumes,
of emissions from faulty systems,
there's been a corner filling station
on every morning, evening, and afternoon
ready to see that I would make it there.

In Beaumont, at Florida St. and Highland Dr.,
the brick building built in nineteen-five
still houses in front the Brothers' Gulf
and out back the home where the one lived then
when his oldest daughter took her holy vows
after the tennis star who would never fail

to rattle on for hours of nothing really new,
the telephone switched from ear to ear
of her teenage smell, married someone else.
For lunch the other brother would walk a block,
his wife preparing pasta and sweet fennel
or the goose their son and I had legally shot.

So high, only the honking would let us know
the V's were over town, heading south to feed
on rice the harvest combines left behind.
Eating them, we dropped buckshot onto plates,
the wild taste cooked out by an Italian recipe
my mother never learned and I'd as soon forget

I ever furnished its ingredients. Instead, I'd have
the Legislature outlaw every gun. But then, we
all sneak up, even on ourselves. Muddy, from

keeping low, we'd work our way on elbows
until the flock, thick and noisy on the ground,
was close enough to stand and shoot. Bloody—

our limit bagged, held by long, warm necks—at sun-
set we'd return, my spirits heavy as the sticky birds,
yet knowing that without a share in the kill, I'd miss
the meals, his mother's baggy hose, his father's
prayers, and all but me crossing themselves.
Could be she really did love Jesus just as well.

To Dr. Fred Logan, Jr., in Hell

(1939-1970)

Bourbon, Schubert, and Illinois, this
is how I am: boozing to romantic mush
states away from the Mexican-American,
Texas town of Mathis and the Chicano
cemetery there, where, weeks ago, they
tamped you down at just my age, planted
with a band you'd doctored, drunked with
to the chagrin of every gringo businessman.

My argument's this: I beat it out of
Hebbronville, before they ran me off.
You, you were free, uncontracted by a
white balding school board. Besides,
even speaking better English, their wage
stayed low as ever. So what good'd it do them
having a teacher with a bachelor of arts
when the bean price weren't no poem?

It falls apart, and I know it.
M.D. or B.A., the degree don't
make the man. I lasted nine months,
and, oh, / The difference to me!
Just look at all it's meant:
another tongue to taste life with,
a wife and son with Latin blood,
a blend that blesses Babel.

Then what would you suggest,
that I go back, get my own shot off
the way that deputy done to yours?
Come on, they're used to it now.
Their 3rd-rate culture of song & dance
been raped by every manifest destiny's

tore through towns of sun & sand
these last three hundred years.

Never even met you, and here I am
talking like the best of friends,
you gone on to patching up some
dumb bastard down below, got himself
bounced out of the pearly gates, for a
bottle of *Cuervo* tried smuggling in
in a worn hip pocket of his western jeans.
Go ahead, admit it, you volunteered again.

Jazz God & Freshman English

Harold T. Meehan

from the day you entered the band hall
needing a 3rd-chair trumpet to take Wayne's place
when at the time I was sitting eleventh in line
my hearing ever since hasn't been the same

prayed for real that every better player
would turn down that lowest of parts
practiced only before or after classes
for the one big blast each spring & fall

not counting the autumn Friday nights
for football sock hops on lips so shot
from marching & blowing half-time shows
till at last you arrived at the awaited name

o perfect you never were
far from it the way you'd breathe
after a soccer game of fifty minutes
winded by all the fags you'd puff

or once on leaving your jumbled home
quietly without a word the record going
you on the couch passed out from mixing
vodka with the bebop licks of Dizzy & Bird

when the couples wanted the band should do
current hits like Elvis's "Hound Dog"
you'd give them "Stars Fell on Alabama"
& plenty of whispered go-to-hells

after band rehearsal of dull Irons & Sousa trios
you'd offer the miracle of Beethoven's 1st
the puzzling wartime 5th of Shostakovich
even *Lust for Life* with Quinn & Douglas

that film seen the night you drove over to
your student's home you the string & stage-
band teacher a grown man inviting imagine
a pimply-faced sophomore seated last chair

to be lowered together down creaking mines
to tulip rows sprouted from oil paint tubes
squeezed by some guy unheard of till then
some Vincent Van Gogh sliced off his ear

then classics through the bore of a Bach 7 C
as lips touched to life that metal mouthpiece
a Martin horn unlocked by your magic key
would open up a world of unending sound

o invitation to more than music or movie
from sunflowers ragged on canvas stalks
but a page's thickness to Blakean lines
where they hang heavy in his two quatrains

his words would release to dreams of love
to the writing & revising deep in the night
for appearance in the obscure magazines
closed down as would be South Park High

& the grade
o yes had almost forgotten
the course went for
no credit

Rev. Elwood J. Birkelbach

no recliner no rocker
could hold you still
your back ever in pain
your brain so restless

as when it worked into a Sunday sermon
Goethe's transcendent image of God

asleep in the earth & in stones until
He dreams in flowers & awakes in man

your second floor study so dark & heavy
with the books & books on the inscrutable Will
Brother Lawrence's letters Luther's reforms
Aquinas & Wesley & the mental health guides

climbed to you up stairs another Mount Sinai
or Kierkegaard's mountains in Moriah
in the pulpit you'd appear a burning bush
sweating & swaying & reddening with

the remembered weight of steamy nights
on South Sea isles your tours in World War Two
as chaplain to troops there after the Jap
your German-Texas ears made captive by

the tale of a tribe transposed itself
from Brazil or Venezuela
retaining in miniature
the nation's shape

as it landed in the blue Pacific
made safe from alien spears
finding peace through telepathy   but never you
always shifting in comfortless armchairs

in the end seeking relief in an insurance firm
from a body & mind
too huge for a church
shrunk by the tithes that bind

Professor Francis E. Abernethy

propped on a classroom desk
the lace work boots never quite going with
your youthful face & the old man's tie
nor with your talk of Sputnik & a Cellini brag

39

nothing in your office
ever quite matched
a Beowulf drawing beside
rattlesnakes curled in glass

Mickey Spillane in one breath
Jonathan Swift in the next
then off on field trips spelunking
or taping folk tales from sixteen-three

ballads surviving
from Shakespeare's day
in sleepy towns like Kountze, Sour Lake or
Buna

no Mahon nor native pecan
yet a Texan from the Piney Woods
& so would set you down
here as if in gumbo earth

that you give again
of caves that throng
with serpents & song
of stalagmites turned to satellites

your heroes old & new
coming & going
in cow-caked Justin kangaroos
quoting Benvenuto

Taking Stock

2nd

Miss Harvey
of the heavy wooden desks
with seats shaped to skinny cheeks
up one flight—2nd grade on the 2nd floor

a rising bodily to new heights new horizons
reading & writing the promise she gave
but where did she go
at end of day

in her dark print dresses
wine or navy blue
her sagging face
of an ashen cast

long window shades lowered for naps
heads down on hard ink-welled tops
sums & subtractions copied from boards
but no such keys would let us in

to that room where no sun came
where the black cat curled
on velvet & sequined couch
an asbestos log fired by the cold gas flame

as she rocked & marked our pages
torn from Big Chief tablets
dreaming of doctors & lawyers
of the PhDs her labor would bear

of the poet would deliver
her Cinderella soul
from that stepmother & her fat-footed daughters
night   insomnia   regret

4th

introduction to Spanish
another language
& love
the same

her notes passed
whenever the teacher
would turn her head
an approximation

yet as close
as any can come
the accent always
giving away

none native to
that land where
flowers blossom
out of season

where birds
will sing without
expecting
spring to stay

*   *   *

as pitcher at recess
felt handsome & fit
with all the right stuff
chosen for the team
on which was just
beginning to belong
then left behind
Suzy too who saved a place
next to hers
in the dining hall

but most of all
that mole by lips
of a face whose name
got lost in the move
its smooth olive cheeks
unkissed in the cloak room
not even off-stage
when we waited in the wings

from the mimeographed program
of those forever have had a part
hers the leading role
in that primary play
or was it more the recognition scene
fear of an end to the act

first love in storage
reclaimed at last
& in memory's care
not so damaged as packed
in a Van Lines crate

María saying rather
it was some special handling for her
but way before
could even guess her spring
or tell it from the star's routine
there had to be
that transfer in winter
to a long low building
an off-white brick
stained russet by the wind-blown sand

its one-story like a continuous first grade
no more graduating to an upper floor's view
seated rather apart
at the back of the room
believing there was nothing
new to learn

picking up habits still haven't dropped
like holding this pen
with the thumb in the air
or worse even
my nose up there

had it been known then
would surely have sworn
had made the Trail of Tears
in a five-hour drive

a short trip north
across the Red River
whose south fork marked off more
than Longhorn from Sooner
into Oklahoma an eyewitness report
as if it had been in fact part of a plan
for now can see how would come to watch
as dad grew into a man
battling alone far from his kin
with bankers & insurance men

selling farmers up to his cuffs in mud
their irrigating tubes flooding the fields
of wheat cotton alfalfa & sorghum
or in the cellar smelled of rotten potatoes
we huddled as a tornado
ripped through the gin

& the unattractive Michigan girl
unattractive as she
two strangers ahead of the class
on that gray afternoon we drove her home
back to the barracks
of Altus' Air Force Base
abandoned those days after the Second War
her father in braces hobbled to the car
his muscled arms & calloused hands
his thin misshapen legs

nothing for a boy but to dream of the past
nothing of beauty in all that land

& though for years it offered no fruit
was yet the setting where this writing took root
& tasteless & green as it keeps coming out
have still to thank that ruddy earth
if what it's about
is salt instead of theatrics

Hustling Shuffleboard With Hearts-&-Flowers Harold

Beeson
better known as the
Beast

from his acned face
& physique
like a bouncer's from across

the railroad tracks
at the College St. Flamingo Club
made all the county beer joints

just after classes
on Hemingway & Faulkner
ordering only *Jax*

that New Orleans
Cajun brew
sprinkling a sandy stuff

on varnished boards
caressing long piano-player's
fingers round a metal puck

sliding it along the flesh-colored
wood back & forth a bit
getting the feel & angle

to hang it off the edge
or give the sucker's a
click would send it

sailing for the gutter
take him for a 5 or 10 spot

high-tailing it out of there

if & when the guy wised up
& decided all of a sudden
to go for a gun

or like the night
a dozen rough-necks
off the tower shift at Spindletop

went for him in sawdust
after he'd crunched a cheater's ribs
up against a washbowl

on the humid wall
of that house converted
to a cockroach bar

or shot through the underarm
on running from a sheriff's raid
out the backdoor to

sweetgum & pine
what little he made
going for booze

& poetry books
elected J.P. in
of all places

Rose City, Texas

Bobby Layne: Quarterback

never led Horns Lions or Steelers with padded hips or a faceguard
never threw a wobbly couldn't count for six & spell the sound defeat
never barked signals but to win those stakes can never take & hoard
never failed to believe in a stadium where no try falls incomplete
never huddled except to call the play would go the distance for History
never went to an audible at the line that a white dove didn't descend
never knew the sweat of spring training as anything short of Glory
never lost a rout or a squeaker just the clock had run out on him
now lazies about on the porch or tosses on another mesquite log
now camps with fellows couldn't care less was or wasn't a champion
now listens as mourning doves feed & mate out in the sand & sage
now wouldn't trade his TV rocker for a fourth & twenty-one
now leaving the bombs to uninspired arms cleans & oils his 16 gauge
now off in post-oak woods pisses on the fire & whistles up the dog

Poem in Time of Drouth

Used to, wood-stove shacks just littered one side.
That or run out of town on a rail. Caused Duke to write
"Across the Track Blues." Could have. Like wind itself
zephyr wheels picked up seed, puffed it out along the right-

of-way, sowed the rift with rare species, weedy "Indian
paintbrushes" & sacred blood of the bearded buffalo,
transplanting races back to beginnings in the sand,
in turn shipping herds East to slaughter in Chicago.

How deny his history's tied to the midnight whistle blowing
solemn across the trestle? Mine and all America's too.
From where I reckon, we've come a damn fur piece. Just returning
three generations back to a sand-blown junction, words & trees were few,

men switched engines "easy" as jobs, willed stopped watches
& intolerance that kills. After thirty-odd years railroading out of Baird,
granddad retired, tried his spotted hand at running a domino hall,
where not a slug nor a bet permitting, he declared

it all a sin, so dad says, who as a boy did his dead-
level best to warn him, "Not a soul will patronize
so prim a place," for all his trouble got a knot on the head.
And sure enough, along with the business, granddad shooed the barflies

off. But there hasn't been any age without its fair share
of running to make a wrong connection, the train
timetable reading such & such, but that one out of date,
much as the style I'm riding in, beside this steamed-up pane.

Yet in the end bull-headed men have brought the bison back,
neighbors of color have hopped a far better fate.
Certainly worry over who's to pay, yet now & again slow 'er up
to let the old wood tower's rainwater slake.

George Catlin & the Horned Toad

There is that about the disbeliever
in what I see out by the ant bed daily,
its hold lost on me, as on foreign fashion the beaver's
was, backtracks thought to when, way before Bailey

teamed with Barnum, P.T. pitched them, no pennants,
not even a tent, barking out of the byword
a fool is born as often as minutes,
making a mint off George Washington's black wet nurse

thirty years post his mortem at 161! With General Tom Thumb,
the midget, he set sail to humbug England,
advertising the troupe's expenses, a hot medium,
at half Jumbo's cost, of a cool ten grand.

Innocent fraud he called it all,
for what's known day in, day out
dulls. Peasants would be wheedled by medieval
minstrels, jugglers, a world to doubt.

Yet home from all disputing, I find the frog's incredible,
a BC creature, antique-skinned, performer of feats
mortality can vie with any storied of a Hannibal:
fifty years in a cornerstone, & alive without eats!

Catlin: Frank Buck of my own clime,
he who brings the toad & Apache back,
back to a lean-to, to a keeping time
with the chant two sing facing each. For exact-

ly on the beat, the obsidian flake's
held in the one's soft, left, elastic
palm, struck by the other without a break
in the arrowhead's shape, a striking in of music,

mystery, a medicine for the chase. Scene
I would never have seen, no rhythm I would have rued,
beauty of death in hands of rarified red men,
through it coming here to see the hippies frug,

this day's aphrodisiac dances, done with
psychedelic lights, a flashing of lines on band & all,
ritual that war-paints love, life a twisted withe
holding a horn-stone for forming a handle

to fashion a flint, designed, destined to fly
& find the heart, minds bent on a letting
of blood, no freedom for the sake of, but survi-
val in my own time, & here I sat, regretting.

Forum on the Mapuche

for Francisco Otta & Bernardo Berdichewsky

We're all Chileans. But what to do with the Mapuche?
An Indian within and without the State.
This is the question we're to look into:
What to do with the Mapuche?
We begin by asking how he sees you and me:

Are no Mapuche.
Our name mean men of earth.
Before you came, only Mapuche knew land.
Teach our tongue, hear our history,
then you understand.

I applaud your pride, but such a world-view
we must designate ethnocentric.
We anthropologists study long and hard
in digs of your bones and your ancient homes
to identify the flute of forgotten songs.
We label yours a subculture, but never to offend,
for we admire your people, alive or found in shards.

What we want is white men gone,
a Mapuche Republic with President.
Then we return to crimeless day,
for Mapuche more moral than your sermon call for.

Ten years I've lived at the Indian's hearth;
childless myself, they've grown like my own.
At night the family encircles the fire;
o that we children were listening there now
to tales of Vulture and the copihue flower.

I mostly am pleased by houses you build,
but smoke of our cooking drive us out.

52

Cold come in through your ready-made wall,
and we can't forget from day to day,
the one key we are given is of a set.

No smarter, no dumber;
no quicker, no slower;
a man with a mind and a heart.
Start by letting him choose *his* way.
Don't push; he's a mule if you do.
And so you'd be, German, Jew or Soviet.

It's been our pleasure at this roundtable talk
having you join with us here.
Our hope would remain that in days to come
we may gather to hear young poets in Mapuche
reading their visions and myths to a drum
recovered by the scientist's spade.

Pérez

Why did Humpty-Dumpty fall?
-He was careless on the wall.
Why didn't all the King's
bad horses and horsemen
put him back together again?
- No one can put an egg together again.
PÉREZ COULD!
Pérez: stripeless overalls,
barefoot in black leather low-quarters,
a mechanic's cap, silently repairing
the commodes and curtains
in the apartments where his
Chilean granny makes her home.

Pérez the Great, fixer of shells
and all the cracks in a fragile world
where a child piles precariously up
his plastic bricks, his Lincoln logs,
and the grand performance
of a sockless custodian
patching a nursery rhyme.

Tonight:
wielding a tinker toy baton,
he mounted and swayed on his Texaco truck,
at his honest-to-goodness music stand
with the wrong score upside down,
a Beethoven string quartet,
and conducted a recording of Bruckner's 4th,
4 years old,
beating time,
defeating all the naughty wolves,
inspired by his one true *maestro*:
the word italicized because
it means to him in Chilean

54

what Pérez is,
a janitor who,
from toilet bowl to Mother Goose,
can symphonize the works.

        O could I I would have
every line in Spanish,
since that's the tongue
his hero Pérez holds,
and the one my illiterate poet
played it in
to his teddy bear's applause.

Divorce

1

like rabbits yanked out
of thin air
the kids arrive to see
what all was never joined
sit in weightless wonder
before a slipping knot
the trapdoor of a magic hat
too soon coming to know
the act done & over
with only the world outside
impressed by sleight of hand
while they must learn
the end of luck
hear a twisting of words
leading up to
the very unraveling of love
that last flight of doves
out of the empty tin
believed in
even after the moon turned dark
when from the first her tinted
lips breathed no other meaning
than touch

2

came weeping
a grown man
said she wanted
to break it off

was glad
but would console him all the same

saying she'd change her mind
yet for his sake hoping not

till when she did
& they were one
still told myself she wasn't
good enough not for Jim

& so back to where all along
had felt it should have been
only then confided in this friend
had feared it would never last

3

remembering it he said
at the wedding
nothing went right

her fat uncle
opened the hood
looked like he was

trying to jerk out the
plugs to stall them in front
of her family's church

jumping out of the car
he yelled you sonofabitch
get your ass away from there

found him trying his best
to bust a champagne bottle
across the radiator cap

their last day together
though they planned it out
the circle closed the

same old way everything
he said went wrong
marriage never was their song

4

two weak strands
won't hold a thing
but one another
though that's not quite
what he meant to say

so he tried again
two weak strands
pull each other down
a metaphor he'd read
always falls apart

but tried once more
two weak strands
aren't so good as
one that's really strong
though he knew alone

neither would ever make it
yet rather than
try again he gave it up
& let his thinner life
lift a lighter load

5

who knows what it takes
who considers the stakes

who burns
who shivers

the one having up its sleeve
a trick or two: to remain

button-mouthed
& blameless

while flame leaps free
of the dry & the gray

catching to neighboring woods
with a pulp of promise

though both lie leery now of the cape
routine
of faith in this box with swords & saws

where only on stage & screen
do partners come out unmarked

6

but even knowing
at any instant
the enchantment could soon wear off
the wand's effect give out
that her one nightmare
of Jofré's return
may still come true
once his good-looks all have flown
with the younger set each year older
less taken with his charms
the beaches in Brazil unbecoming
to his spindly legs & ebbing hair
come tottering back in
like nothing ever happened
so sure the Catholic Church in Chile
will recognize him just the same
& though Gladys knew his game

she wanted a pair after their first girl came
so held him close again
for love of her I'd wed
& even knowing that had he come
to find her in my arms
base blood in his own home
this alchemy could never have been
my gratitude goes out to Rio
to whatever bed he's in
blessing him for this marriage cup
Milton the True Magician
has proven in puritan prose
so full it overflows

Auction

At the first farmhouse to the right,
on the blacktop north of Creston,
the auctioneer has his p.a. mike
wrapped with a rag, strapped to his chest, on

and ready to trill them out, to shout our bids
till the Brunswick player with a busted arm,
the blue-onion plates so cracked and chipped,
the rusted pots and harness, fresh out of horse and barn—

every bargain's been amplified, upon this open air.
As under the oaks and elms, looking in the grass more
like wounded troops, their caissons rolled up here and there,
the buggies and beds lie scattered now, the corn-

fields all around standing futile guard against
this Illinois fall, advancing in among the sale,
attaching with its mist to items by the fence:
a wooden bath of casket shape, needing only a lid nailed

down, spirit seemingly sucked out its unplugged drain;
the piles of books on marketing hogs, federal laws,
Dickens' English history, Lee of Virginia; the chains,
boots, and utensils; the going, going, gone—off

in strangers' cars, away in collectors' trucks,
to where their lives may or may not find
an eternal home filled with love;
their accumulated days, an attic safe from time.

At the Foodstamp Center

staring at questionnaires
as she awaits her turn
the divorcee dreams
of lettuce leaves

not pale green forms
with question marks
like worms working
a garden patch

while caseworkers digging in
read up on what poverty means
popping their diet colas
tossing tabs to the trash

scaling the gar in file 13
where into its dark whirling
waters the black peers down
to catch a swirling of channel cats

to believe he has a bite
a hold on a long cane pole
the sound feeling
of coffee grounds

in cans now filled
not with blanks or dotted lines
but red ribbed squirmings
fit for hooks which

just as they ask the living stream
are answered by
a cork that dances
a reel that sings

Directions for Getting Here

Out of DeKalb
at the first and
our only filling station
hook a left.
With all your windows down
the fertilizer smell
will hit you
coming in from the
cornfields off to the
right where the sun
will just be beginning to set.
Go on past the township's lone patrol car,
green and sitting at home
while the husband's inside
grabbing a bite of fresh garden delights.
Watch for kids, they'll all be out,
their Mason jars lit with lightning bugs.
The signal flashing or not
stop at the tracks
and feast your eyes on the paintless station,
its weeds, rusting wheels, and MALTA
in fading black and white.
Cross on over the rails
and catch a right on Adams St.,
a chug-holed road
with its quaint brick library
catty-corner and closed
half the nights.
Bend
on around by the Purina Chows'
red and white checkered feed mills.

Take the first road again on your right,
with the gray, dry-walled two-story house
where the big pine spreads an inviting scent
but the signs on the fencing warn:
"No Parking," "Beware of Dog,"
"Meteor a Shooting Star."
At the very next gravel drive,
sparrows there
defleaing themselves in the dust,
turn on in. Most folks
not from these parts
swear this town's only fit
for the hogs our local
farmers raise,
but we've as yet to find
more wrong here
than anywhere.
So come on by, bring your poems along.
We'll have the beer iced down,
the fire started,
everything ready
when y'all arrive.

Reading the Sun

(Santiago de Chile)

Ever local in nature
each work opens
on rooftops & trees
of a feature
fitting the nation.

Author for a day
of the place to
which it warms,
even now, with early
morning, it's passing

the political rally,
rolling as a trolley bus
silently by,
flashing when a
line connects,

casting comments
off a speaker's specs:
light! –
for what utility
the land elect.

Claudio Arrau on Public Television

at seventy years
he's not coming in so well
though the fault is none of his fingers

rather it's this interference
come to his "Appassionata"
from another channel's bloodless stream

disparate waves rolling in
to the antenna at
a 60-mile remove from

the PBS transmitter
weaker than a network beam
yet in between distortion

& typical phrases of the day
"a high of 88 a low of 55"
the veined hands of this Chilean man

speak of Tierra del Fuego
chord as southern cascades
lift ranges snow-capped & smoking

turn cold ivory into volcanic tremolos
erupt as if from the announcer's mouth
spewing the facts with revealing runs

weather reports struck by thunder claps
shut-outs : the season's first no-hitter
fanned by flames from

1806 : the black & white set
yellowed & roiling
in a Beethoven blaze of light

as stiffening joints
pound fire & flood
into the Nightly News

Confessions of an Imperialist Poet

my virile ways amaze me so:
at times an invisible moth
chewing holes in their pants & shirts

instead of providing arch supports
heels snug-fitting & enclosed
for workers' toes & mud-cracked soles

I strap their feet to General Tire
suck the fruit trees dry
inflate the currency lower the streams

to where current is cut that runs the pumps
accept their insults as only just
even thrive on curses & slanderous lies

take full credit for the incompletion
of home or office supply
pleasure in bent rods rising from unfinished tops

of windowless walls or if at all
their only paint white crosses on panes
with political signs as substitute

for working the job straight through
the siesta a national disgrace
though arriving ulcerous I'd much rather rush

in the market meanwhile I buy not a thing
steal off with whiffs from the pepper-hot meats
green tortillas tangerines neatly in stacks

on other days send my Chilean wife
their finest Latin treasure I took
right from under their brown-eyed looks

to shop for breads to bargain & haggle them down
to lower prices for making a meal
will feed a gringo with sky-blue eyes

on Sundays ascend to the Aztec pile
a pyramid topped with a cathedral in Spanish style
take in the valley below its patchwork fields stake out

reaping the maize with my gaze bent like butterflies
lighting to lift the nectar & scent
though on stamen or pistil no pollen remains

raping the image of poplar-lined hills
replacing what's taken with sewage & trash
then making the most even of worthless sights

on city streets orange peels & spit
diesel exhaust from unmufflered trucks
buses rusted in want of parts

mangy dogs beggars huddled without regard
at the door of a bolted heart
scene after scene of senseless dirt

all exported for sell to bring in the almighty buck
though more as broken bits of non-profit poems
with rich lines on the lives of the colorful poor

as from this vista can envision the land
dotted with Holiday Inns gothic castles to which

barefoot Toltecs will peddle their wares

hand-woven rugs hammocks & chairs
in exchange from the lordly uncalloused hand
for a pittance of the charge for a thick juicy steak

baked potato with butter chives & sour cream
o can't you taste it now a whole new world
of bourbon central heat & clean white sheets

if only my song can come up to the dream
to sing it would trade off a hundred slow maids
ten ton of burros their masters thrown in for free

The Frame Maker

We go to him on the Day of the Dead
when marigolds mark the eucalyptus trees
where buses pinned loved ones to bleed,
find his booth at the market indoors,
rife with the smells of bubbling vats,
dried fish hung up, open charcoal fires,
and the florist's oval funeral wreaths,
overly sweet so near to his shop
where dozens of crucified Christs
hang crowned from crosses of assorted shades,
some with plain, most with mirror finishes,
reflecting the thorned heads over and over,
while displayed out front, ready in frames,
is our Lady of the Tough or Desperate Case,
and next to her, the hand of her Son,
in its pale white palm that crimson slit,
his fingers spread to a cloud above
where four haloed saints stand posed
in attitudes holy, in brightly-colored robes,
a child alone on the rung below,
his left hand raised in sign of peace,
holding in his right a globe,
and beside this another gaudy print
portrays at the corners miniature scenes,
variations on its center-piece Virgin,
like the Mexican bandit's escape,
till he turns in the desert and over his shoulder
catches or is caught by her vision there
suspended in rainbow waves, her hands
as ever together in prayer.
We, we're looking down at all of these,

but our real business remains with the man
whose specialty is religion and its memories,
though has not attended mass for months,
making certain his concern's a go.
When asked, we stammer the order out,
surprised at what shame our voices reveal:
gold frames for Currier & Ives,
a diploma for this, a degree for that,
earthly rewards we come to regret
we could ever achieve or accept,
when the maker of frames
brings us happily back
to the facts of glue and glass,
his cross-cut saw in a measuring vise,
his cutter that squeaks as he draws,
then mysteriously snaps the perfect fit,
a cut near as fine as the one where a nail
pierced the sinew and line of a life.

Lines & Mounds

writing letters of words
on those authors' outsized
American poems they now
take shape upon the page

like their Nazca lines
they incised in sand
like their Hopewell mounds
formed of fertile earth

with the m's & n's
as if burial grounds
for a cult of vowels
caught & held

between the bones
syllables to rub
against the roof
to click the teeth

or crook the tongue
sticking to lips
until their souls
escaping the mouth

may fly & mix
with sun & sky
their soft open sounds
may move the valleys

to make reply:

a's & e's & i's
the o's & u's
like polished stones

an alphabet washed on
shore & meaning what
its colors declare
its veins belonging to

lost mountain mines
the conjugation of an
ocean verb the liquid l's
& r's as if cascaded down

from Andean peaks
tumbled by melting snow
to lie at the Pacific foot
of the *Tree of Life*:

six-hundred & two feet high
three yucca-like limbs
dug in the sandhill cliffs
of the Paracas Bay

pointing to the Pisco Plain
with its A.D. 500
desert poems of Perú
its *pair of hands*

holding the ball of land &
sea its *snake-necked bird*
forever in flight far
from the Empire State

or a White House in need
of more than Peacock paint
the nation heavy with a dirt
fallen from political winds

storms such moltless feathers take
in or out of favor or here closer
to our Illinois home plenty starves
for want of that workman-

ship in flint the Indian dead
took to their deathless graves:
turtle carapaces
shells & copper plates

embossed instead of dates
with timeless crafted lines
reading: a buried art rising
on wings of Wisconsin mounds

Serpent Mound

(Louden, Ohio)

dark December's leafless trees
stretch their thin & shadow lines
upon your winding quarter a mile
shed of its summer green

your skin yellowed & unshining
your jaws no longer taking in
a grassy egg but rather now
the cold oval of winter

or as the Hopi tradition holds
a mud mound standing for
the Snake Clan village
protected by your power

in any season you symbolize
more than all the rest
by dint of being of the greatest length
of any serpent anywhere

yet instead of sin you mean
one in touch with palpitant earth
living as you do beneath her leaves
under her rocks knowing their weight

finding your strength in her decay
coiling about with a love-death squeeze
would make us spit out the oil of deceit
& save us from a burning in night

Spider

the hawk in the highest tree
the condor atop the apex rock
the eagle gliding against the sky
all fall to your fragile web

every lesser wing of wasp or fly
lashed to masts of silken threads
sails with you through wind & rain
a sea with stars of morning dew

great & small you catch at last
in your patient innards art
your gastric juice geometry
exact & sticky as the thought

of death in wait beneath the flight
return to earth from heaven's hills
exchange of vistas for mist & fog
of sun's gold for candle's counterfeit

finding you underfoot others see you weak
but all along these knew you strong
that the proud gone up must in the end
settle for this: listening to the widow weave

& so here in the desert they drew you
with lines for your legs acres long
out of all proportion yet as true to reach
as daylight come to dance your tune

Leviathan

an elegy for Pablo Neruda

O makers you surely had him in mind
yet even you with such majestic maps
that mysterious way of shaping the fan
of a tail would chart the stars

could not have guessed so extensive a range
as this singer's residence & ode
but choose you did the measure meet
metaphor of the man would sound your land

though still you missed the mark
as all have fallen short
for to do him justice would call for
jaws seemingly at rest / upon the ocean floor

while above where the albatross shadows
his cross upon the curving waters
a geyser would need to shower the waves
& desert grooves how could they grow

a fruit brought forth from the sea
as out of his depths the likenesses towered
an ambergris melon submerged in summer's grass
the making of such similes taking at the very least

a hemisphere of comforts & howls
for even to his hurricane reaches
the Mediterranean would only equal
but a drop in a galactic lake

any comparison turning finally absurd
as Wyatt & Surrey's hyperboles
where sick with elephantiasis were
their lovers' renaissance sighs

& thus so huge is the praise he's due
unwieldy the hulk I've tried to sail
for a sighting of Chile's poet-whale
that at last I enter this nutria slough

& stepping on bank of Cow-Cow bayou
find the cattle tracks more my size
hoof prints & hay cakes easier on eyes
than readings underneath / beyond the skies

a safe return to the Texas coast
the shoals & shallows of home
but like Plato's enlightened soul
blind from that black fire swallowed schools

come back to sense in the horse manure
an image of meteor & moon
a fresh green pile changed utterly
though the terrible American beauty is gone

yet still he leads us on through a tunneled celery sea
up to the apogee of its green lineal lightning
on from there to Macchu Picchu / aerial mate
to the Nazca lines / only his own more heightening

María's Lamp

we desperately needed one
to see to eat her suppers by
the borrowed house left un-
furnished we couldn't buy

an expensive type ready-made
beds more pressing she'd decide
we should purchase just a shade
for its base would use a purified

water bottle & I *I* should
fix it all! with her confidence
driving me on I did what I could
but cut wires short rents

in everything my temper
touched swore I couldn't do it
tore outside to whimper
wanting so to be a poet

not a stupid handyman
returned without a poem
but loving her a better plan
for how to illumine our home

rewired refitted & taped
to her green transparent glass
(as if some verse I'd shaped)
a fixture made of brass

then tightening the socket saw
as the pliers were catching hold
a gripping image of how to draw
& fasten such paradox as old

as nighttime plainer than day
with bulb casting clarity off the ceil-
ing paint watched it on the table lay
a lake of light for our evening meal

Tornado

1

   a funnel drops
swirling from its
   cell
in summer air

   warm
bath water
   down
what drain

2

   the hundred-watt bulb
without a river to burn
   we watch by watering wax
by charring wick

   patterns the house plants make
their shadows growing
   folded to the ceiling
swaying with the flame

   hear Bach by candlelight
his Art of Fugue
   through the battery-powered
FM set

   another storm
his composed near death

raging even dimly there
where in bed the tapers

    lit him
his feather pen
    one wing cast
clapping upon the wall

3

    out to witness its wake
cars pass as in procession
    for that rare trip to the plot
no grave-side game just the curious
    driving to see where the radio warning
turned real & entered town

interrupting dull routines
    broke off circuits & heated words
twisted trees & TV towers
    stopped the hours
flooded basements on giving
    longer pause
to the periodic hum
    the distant thunder
of sump pumps coming on
    safe needed sound
from underneath

now in the streets
    phone lines & maple limbs
in one another's arms
    improper lovers
gone to bed

caught with
no way to call & report
    such outrage to
Mayor or County Board

4

    all the next Illinois day
a rattling whirr
    blue clouds & fumes
of chain saws
    bringing them down
the split & shattered years

    in village history
its soft hearts & shading leaves
    corded logs
for long winters
    of icy eyes & colder touch

5

once domed & corrugated
    the feed mill
    wadded up & blown away

what fresher image
    the author
    had in mind!

in its metal stead
    a heaped poem
    open to a bluer sky

with its golden grain
   high & bright
   over which a

cloud of field
   birds now
   circles to descend

A Wedding Sestina

Everyone inside is dressed up pretty as a picture,
though none of us can manage what the bride
will, without her even trying. White-gloved ushers seat us, as piano
strains set an uninspiring mood, the flowers on the altar
wilting in this warm Southwestern afternoon, when the groom
will do it, four months late. Gathered, all await the vows' repeating.

Up front, the pathetic-but-happy-girl-friend-of-a-pianist goes on repeating
what she was asked to play. An aunt, perhaps, snaps her picture
with Kodak insta-matic. The soloist, some cousin to the bride,
holds her music up, clears her throat, and, askant the altar,
nods three times before the girlfriend at the battered piano
discovers she's ready to pour forth song, out upon groom

and congregation. For now, down the aisle between best men, the
        handsome groom
ambles to where the singer sings and aunt stands aiming to take his picture.
Behind the flashing cubes, on this 2nd Baptist Church's bare-walled altar,
a patch of cement crudely glares at us, just as the same piano
piece, begun again, seems, in its unashamed, wrong-note way, repeating
what's awkward here today. And now she bangs an entrance for the bride.

Preceded by a pig-tailed sister and a beaming brother to the bride,
their outfits bright as the building's dull, the mother-to-wed's a picture,
her race's, proud despite the crud's been done her, head high, facing the
        altar
where sex will be approved, her love in need of no repeating.
And smiling in his winning way, dancingly, though quite stoned still, the
        groom
gets set to turn the blues to a "Milenburg Joys" for jazz piano.

With bride and groom joining hands before the sober pastor, the pitiful
        piano
silent now, I see the heavy faces, not this way from a belated repeating,
but just because they got here black. How happy yet the picture!
For under burdens on their brows, a prideful hope for the trembling bride
and her big man breaks out like the grin on a derby winner's groom,
as rings like wreaths are slipped on fingers swelling at the fanless altar.

The vows exchanged, the sermon at an end, the couple descends altar
steps to the pallid music played again on the out-of-tune piano.
But harmony has been performed today, for this is what repeating
is, and so the aunt can run ahead to shoot the sacred picture.
Filing out now with all the rest, I search about for my friend the groom,
seated in a black sedan, tied with cans, rice on him and on his bride.

Reaching out the window, the groom shakes hands, as we go on and on
        repeating
"Best of luck," "Don't stay up too late," all the cleverness a blushing bride
expects. Altar empty, piano shut, baby in another car, that's about the
        picture.

Two Texas Poets Rendezvous at the Bowie Public Library

Summer: the climate dry
the county too
no relief not a billboard's

beer ad's mountain springs
on coming in from Cowtown
"Out Where the West Begins"

out where the wetness ends
where it all begins
the love & hate all over again

the meeting Hoggard heading here
to this Hudson Bay midway between
Fort & Falls / Worth & Wichita:

cities that saw our two tongues born
as if the Colonel's knives
in bayou gaming fights

so cutting to
the unsuspecting couples gave them birth
their babes turned vegetarians & worse:

versifiers in a land of steak & leather
parents so pained by the fun would make
of all their sacred cows

our sandals a sacrilege still
ours the hides they'd tan to within

an inch of our godless lives

beards turning them in narrow graves
& as we drive slowly across the state
our herds of matinee memories raise

clouds of half-regret
then enter this genesis town
a Gary Cooper showdown

but in place of six-guns
slung at hips
our latest manuscripts

publications drawn out friendly-like
from briefcase & manila folder
on the table poems spread like poker hands

leaning back two trappers fully clothed
floating on this air-conditioned carpet
a green lake in early spring

would-be mountain men who fountain up
spray one another with
metaphor & myth

trading titles of little mags:
Coyote's Journal
Granite Noose Prairie Schooner

long winter tales
of the big one missed
(a sonnet nearly taken)

the librarian's frozen looks
thawing some
at the sound of Frost & Yeats: bubbling brooks
that had they come

to these sizzling western streets
the posse would have found
their desperado words as hard to handle
as flashfloods in mid-July

at the café where we lunch
all around is talk of rain
sighted east of Saginaw
though the only darkening to reach this far

a pair of strangers
dare to eat here hairy & all
like Blacks still out
after the sun has set

& yet because love breaks the strictest laws
we leave a generous tip
despite what reason recommends
& the tide of hatred this quiet town's recalled

Mural on Old Jail Wall / Mora / New Mexico

1

A lion drawn in charcoal
an animal the inmate never saw
its square menacing jaw
its massive shaggy mane
rousing his cell to circus life
by the stare of beady eyes & black nose shaped
like Aladdin's lamp shedding what light
on thoughts of apocalypse vengeance or escape?

2

Proving himself no *mariposa* / no square
was herded in & slammed behind bars
sentenced to facing four bare walls
or traded open air for three squares a day
found filling though not so vital as when
after punching cows or riding fence
the ranch-house triangle was heard
to clang out time for chowing down

3

So four long fangs now form a cube
two above two below feeding his hungry head
four smaller incisors add a box within that box
everywhere black squares the thick tongue one
the paw another with its four nailed claws
a pollex higher breaks the pattern
yet even the mane parted & hanging
is a three-sided square of hair

4

Incarceration reflected through art's release
no full-grown beast on all fours
but a square become a fearsome jaw
its figure a clear-cut threat
or an order out of chaos
to what purpose what nightmare?
right-angled to what desire?
gnashing of decision & inner fire

5

By day the cat half in sun half in shade
beams lower / the bars cast shadow stripes
turn him more ferocious tiger-like
till later moonlight lends a friendly grin
when the artist in his visionary bunk
squints & admires the midnight effect
of a softer glow on the adobe brick
his sketch tamed / his mind the same

6

Four walls but none holds him in
his mattress on one a cushion
a flowerbed with springs of revenge
on a second his window provider of sky
the door a source of wheat & rain
the fourth with this canvas of colors that change
an easel to ease hard knocks blast hates let hot air out
inflate with dread imaginings his tawny carbon skin

7

Would he be ushered into the maw of strength?
pass courageously through the portal jaws?
the ivory pillars open wide with a flash

on the apocalyptic stars of intestinal night
close shut as bars on a grate or cell
his memories conducting to heaven or hell
which will it be? artistry unable to tell
true torment? the waiting it out in the dark

8

Yet looking into the pit he may well see
himself the main feature in uniform on safari
confronting the trials of African grass
torrential floods or locust swarms
safe in his cave subduing tribe after tribe
in shorts as in newsreels from the 1940s
hear as if the roar of Metro-Goldwyn-Mayer
starring handsome him hero one & only

9

Come at last to know his lair's patient lingo
its redemptive talk captive back of the teeth
of this king caged within his cell-block wall
touches thus to his own a tongue rippled & arched
ready as a dammed river of melted mountain snow
to burst over his rocky dental falls
leap into a blazing ring followers proclaim the millennium
or waken deeply from dandelion dreams a drunk sleeping it off

At the Laundromat

"There is no gratitude
in mercy and in medicine." –Gertrude Stein

After losing two dimes
to the coke machine,
her limp to a green lawn chair
exacts return of compassionate times.

On sitting down close
to an unknown friend,
she yanks off a shoe,
grabs hell by the heel,

& with proof in hand,
informs her companion
of a pain that shoots
straight from her bunion.

Pity would have me offer
the relief of a proper fit,
yet relieved to hear
the dryer has stopped,

I load clean clothes
in the laundry bag,
sling its warmth
to the small of my back,

& with sloshing of bleach
go rushing past,
then slow on seeing
both quite at ease,

on hearing them happy
enough to discuss at
length each's ills
for the other's pleasure.

The Poet at Twelve & Twenty-Five

Though what is needed now I haven't got,
there was a time when I could improvise.
In place of store-bought games
I'd drag out my midnight eyes,

see the moon was up,
and take off cross the cotton patch.
That Sooner dog would take right in after
a long-eared rabbit, while all I'd catch

was a clod or two
down tennis shoes. Till then somehow,
through polecat spray,
we'd come to where the farmer's plow

had turned about, the graves began.
It came so natural back in those days
I paid it no mind at all.
Without a thought for where its blaze

might blow, I'd build a fire
from deadwood piled by a barbed-wire fence,
with coyote skins tied drying stiff.
Once that's gone, what's the use in sense?

Keeping Tabs on the Other Guy's Take

For several months' running, both
in dark from that time of birth,
the two musicians played apart,
four cold blocks of Moneda Street
trafficking between their songs.

Today, in the shade, in the shadow
of a branch of the Banco del Estado,
here where for better or worse
harmony's ranks have gathered
arrayed in winter's uniform

of castoff toboggan and army coat,
these blind are warming the banking day
with their fiddle and Spanish guitar,
cups hanging from instrument necks
to catch what coin well-off discard.

And yet can such a union last?
Or shall I, out of good intent,
dropping my trifle
to just one tin,
return each tone

to lonely battle,
when even with eyes
for seeing this sight,
elsewhere envy makes me feel
the beggar again.

A Guided Tour of Granny's Yard

Pardon me hon'. I'll have my
breath just here in a jiffy.
This old lawnmower wears me
near to a nub. Got to where
she's cranky as they swear I
am. Bogs down so

till this grass will be
the death of me.
Now don't you fret yourself one bit.
You just come on over here.
Them there? Why them's dwarf larkspur.
Reddens next to 'em is poppies.

My son's only daughter,
Betty Boop I always call her,
she's the one wanted those.
Planted the spring it was.
I'd brung her back for a visit
from Oklahoma City. Her very

first trip on a train. She stayed on here
couldn't say how long. A month for sure.
They none of them comes anymore.
This messy mimosa's 'bout done for.
Onct it dies I won't put up with anothern.
Drops these brown blooms like

dirty drawers, all over the goldfish pond.
Bad as having males about the house.
Had roomers here in the war. Sailors.

Put a straight-jacket on me at a party.
That oak? Squirrels have a nest
high up in this old hackberry. I s'pose

they's the ones hid the acorn. Yes,
I'm crazy 'bout rocks too. Doodie Bug,
my younger daughter's older boy,
he picked this one up
down at the corner lot.
Said he'd brain me with it

if my bird friends
didn't stop telling me
every wrong thing he'd start to do.
I used to catch him
before he could break the limbs
climbing in that vitex tree.

He always thought they flew
to that redwood feeder and talked to me.
I did to them. Still do, but they . . .
Rushing off so soon? Well honey, come back by
anytime. I'm always here.
Just yell. That bell ain't worked in years.

Five Versions of the Twelfth Street Rag

Duke Ellington & His Jungle Band (1931)

Musician of mystery, orchestrator
of African shades, indigo moods;
by voodoo, right off the bat,
he hexes, derails engine to caboose,

duping dancer & listener. Or swinging
a wand-baton flare, a lantern that switches,
he revoices the very sex of the saxes
to licorice sticks of higher pitches,

uncoupling even Carney's masculine horn
to disguise him Stella, fallen star,
headed straight for Elysian Fields
on board the Stygian diner car:

locomotive the maestro's favorite means
for arriving at Hades unawares–
conductor who never tries putting thought off,
a child caught short of the fare,

for he knows it'll hop a ride, hang outside,
at crossings hear us shrill sirens
roaring to whore the unbelieved-in,
woodwinds as alarm there-is-no-fire-in

hopes held unachieved, will see acts of any sort
all pale passengers come to care for,
though true intentions bear a rootless seed,
carry within their why & own wherefore.

Now alternating his brass & reeds
Duke weaves the way to a junction where
blacks & whites can cross the tracks,
where antiphonal two-pianos will share

the times, cool, toss them forth & back
like hot potatoes or stolen cash:
two years before this take
history records the market crash,

yet song steams mightily on, as Tricky Sam,
oiling it up, a bottle of bootleg beer
halfway up his trombone bell, reels off
Duke's ritual merry-go-round, while Sonny Greer,

fireman this of an imperceptible touch,
keeps on keeping time at boiling,
with Chinese gongs or tin scrub boards,
shoveling a beat as clean as Spring,

a pulsing truth, though ever unuttered,
a sample of Sambo's butter, with strumpets
cooking the feel, stirring up would-be plans
tasty as batter willed undone, trumpets,

with Cootie punctuating among,
now sentencing the soul to speak,
as does an engineering Nanton,
whose tongue is in his cheek,

or now again as pepper hot
as Jelly Roll, Juan Tizol
I meant to say, no Don Juan he,
no not at all, but in the role

to season the rag,
outwit keepers of hell's hot ditch,
pen a sneezing staccato fit
on devilish dolls, tricking them into pitch,

for he's an immigrant valve-trombonist,
born & bred a Puerto Rican,
who thumbs his open notes
at pretense, as at Satan—

Jenkins brakes, the band's a flaming expression,
churning & burning till every brass,
out of Malbowges & back on his knees,
whistle stops it, with three short laughs.

Fats Waller & His Rhythm (1935)

Easy as a Pullman porter's shuffle, or so it sounds,
though heaven-bound he is, & faultlessly pounds
it out. What a rag his! that drags us in,
drops a pun, sins weighty what wasn't,
funny bones mid-flight of a ticklish phrase
shouting as if thought painfully sways
away from Swing to a realer rhythm.
Reached by that run, who wouldn't eat a plum,
apple, anything to laugh off the shafts of
this overture that tells, swears no love
ever missed the mark, confides, "Yore shurta find,"
fumbling the heart & humbling the mind.
Weeping clown at the God-box, loader he of dice:
o fine Arabian reader, hear them both & realize
there's less of Variety in Edmund's lay
& upon what meaningfully Fats could play.

Count Basie & His Orchestra featuring Lester Young (1939)

A spare piano intro, Jo Jones on woodblock.
  Basie's left hand a tribute
  to his old Professor Fats, not then mute,
nor ever should be. Let ages rock,
  swing it out for him
  who made of hilarity another hymn.

Not many notes.
  Well-placed instead.
  Here the other day read
where back East in racial riots
  a black business burned
  when wind turned

round, flew fire back.
  Seeing as how his dollars done died
  took to suicide.
Rare case that, for black has the knack,
  as any color should, to make it right along,
  to rise up over flapping justice on wings of solid song.

Then leap in Lester, bend to your life's own tenor,
  hear in that tone your message,
  receive of a reed its minimum wage,
blow it as the last of Swing's big spenders,
  throwing away those hard-earned cents
  to buy by booze a brighter sense.

But where's the end in that? Where's Dickie Wells, that ham?
  Humor has served you better than grog.
  You've laughed down every demagogue
'tween Natchez & Little Rock, Texas to Alabam'.

Euday's rag may have cracked you up, but then you saw,
as Dada did, how handy a weapon's a good guffaw.

O there it goes, crossing that bridge-like part again,
that clickity rhythm that eggs me on,
keeps me hearing this monotone,
this hankering I have on the brain
for banking on reason's reservoir,
withering hard rows hoed & prayed for.

O memory's rain, why fall so narrow?
Soak my road that I may come by feel
to know how Satch, the Duke, Fats, & Bill,
while plowed & replowed under a harrow,
listened long to the beat of their blood,
at last to make a music, magic as mud.

Beaumont: Class Reunion

1

In a year marked by mountains & mole
hills   awaking each morning
to the real but postcard spectacle

of Popocatépetl   to the petty bribe
& a lawful yet unending heart-
rending romantic-socialist Mexican strike

I sit down unready though desperate to write
of the Golden Triangle where two decades back
as a senior at South Park High

graduation came as a relief   a cocky farewell
like all the rest   though the last attended
other degrees taken   received by mail

though never achievement   its celebration
any feeling   any sense of completion
lost in the onward rush toward some

UFO of the soul   later identified with
the poetic line & what María now calls
a Texas my memory has turned to myth

yet returning after twenty short years
may this private reunion remark how friends
have helped unknowingly shape an imaged ascent

may move them more than inscriptions they read
in the trophy case or that sad yearbook section
where few if any were chosen likely to succeed

2

too talented to give a hot damn
it all came
too easy to care

the beauty queens who called
or hung about as the tennis king
reigned on clay or asphalt court

the nonchalance of his passing shot
or at marching practice on the field
where he hurled his horn in the air

could play it better crumpled up
than those with dentless trumpets
giving it all they had

dressed like the rebel James Dean
with his ducktail & pants pulled low
cigarettes hidden from parents

a meek mother worshipped the earth
where he stepped danced outdid the rest
then gave it all up

took a refinery job like his dad's
the same father whose effusive love
shamed him in front of his friends

married a nobody plain & poor
rented a house happy as hell two blocks
from the home his genius had mocked

3

on tattered wallpaper hang   photos of his father
riding in rodeos pictured atop his champion mount
holding up a blue ribbon in one hand   a *Pabst*

in the other   sitting tall in the saddle   erect
& trim   a far cry from the broken paunchy little man
sits around his matchbox house

with a hernia   his hat on   in pee-stained pants
cursing his dancer son   for some effeminate fool
watches re-runs   Rockettes kicking in crotch-shot

rhythms   no son of mine muttered as he stares to where
the glazed bull horns stretch   above their *Zenith* set
the choreographer-to-be   eyeing the girls in gaudy drill

on downtown streets pauses before the showcase windows
left untrimmed   bare models with contorted limbs
his own in imitation   till he cackles out loud   pirouettes a-

way   clips out scenes from women's magazines
adding a caption to an ad   of two facing kids
the unlikely boy releasing lines   to an innocent mate

"I'll rip those pink panties to a shredded fringe
'round your *Buster Brown* orthopedic saddle oxfords"
a humor horrifies his mother home from the beauty parlor

later to make his name in lights   in old New York
to tour with the Nikolai troupe   to Italy & France
his manikin body ridden   a bronc of modern dance

4

perennial winner as Miss Personality Plus
her limbs & features falling short of feminine
tall & big-boned was leader arbiter Christian

always called on to sing or pray
ever elected the president of society or club
her name synonymous with school spirit & love

though when it came to getting a date
for the Halloween dance hayride or game
her friends were faced with an impossible task

the boys they found willing were never her size
could only come up as far as her chin
in morals not even so high

surprising to all she eschewed a degree
thanked Daughters of Foreign & Revolutionary Wars
but could not accept their scholarship checks

took what her trio of girlfriends had sung
"A Sentimental Journey"   this as an airlines stewardess
fulfilling a Methodist sense of fellowship & service

while the trio remarried & majored in Psych
she flew off to Atlanta Chicago New York
bending to businessmen with stiff drink & a smile

spending her layovers in every big city
rooming with Sappho's jet-age descendants
never once to shed a Mary Magdalene tear

5

in Salem she might have spent time in the stocks
been branded X-rated or charred at the stake
while in Beaumont was more than anything ignored

with her unshaven legs spread like a man's
she sawed out of tune as last violin
though first in soccer beat hell out of all

with petticoats hiked her muscled calves flexed
she outscored & kicked every male in the shins
bowling the Van Winkles over for a go-ahead goal

though her voice hardly raised so any could hear
never absent   never late   faithful to the end
even at the prom her rose corsage failed to wither

as the unknown escort decked in a traditional tux
waltzed her about the ballroom in a low-cut gown
her longish hair by *Toni* or some spray-set brew

yet no medieval change rushed over her then
no frog leaped into being a center-fold bunny
no duckling molted into a kitten for *Gent*

only in Puritan hearts of those who stared
struck by the lightning of their hidden regrets
shamed scarlet by thoughts had lodged & fed

stood judged of a hunting ugly as any
McCarthy managed on the star-chamber floor
sentenced to burn forever for having hoped her a . . .

6

This Is Your Life   a poetry show
brought to you by Paradox & Chance
emceed by Terza   the Star of Stanzas

transportation provided by Imagery Airways
accommodations arranged by Diction & Rhyme
wardrobe courtesy of Symbol Inc.

all the lives were produced & directed
by those who furnished their spirit & form
by teachers whose classes opened & filled

indebted still to those who made it happen
equally to those who made it near impossible
who forced a reconsideration   a renewal of faith

still deeply grateful to each scribbled wall
to bannered steps   lockers bent & pictured
English & typing tests labs & study hall

but most of all owe a special thanks
to those who appeared to bring them back
the screams & tears when the curtain parted

& could see at last the Lives I Led
hear again the storied days they generously gave
hearts had touched mine into feeling

to this & more bid fond farewell
till same teenage hour same graduation
wishing the years to come may enrich as yours

A Little Something for William Whipple

1

back & forth on the crisscrossing walks
building to brick building of then Lamar Tech
changing of classes in a blinding white light
no St. Paul just a coastal summer sun
a choking from the smog & fumes drifting in
from adjacent refinery or the sulfur pits
while reading beneath those stunted loblolly
unreached to rooftops of gravel & tar
all a veritable Garden
at the very least a Texas Eden

where library assignments you made
even now with a Ph.D.
I still wouldn't pass such tests
climb to heights your search required:
newspapers from Boston in '73
an obscure note in French on Edgar Poe
couldn't find them to save my soul
boiling then in your scholarly hell
shoulder to the Sisyphean stone
only to have it roll back down

when in from humid heat to freeze between
the refrigerated stacks & colder stares
from a lady librarian at her reference desk
would try again to discover at last
the why of Doctor Johnson's long fear of death
as a yellow fog engulfed the campus
filled the halls was Heaven to me

& just to breathe the novels
you taught in a huff
worth finishing with a stigma C

2

to your office as to an altar would come
offering the lines like a newborn lamb
as thick with symbols as with wool the ram
till you sheared the fluff   whole stanzas   even the one
arrived so wondrously alive   so miraculously
so mysteriously as when the ewe drops her young
from a study of sonnets had made that innocent song
only to have you leave it standing ugly & unsteady

then found it to be the fittingest gift
when you deigned to slit the bleating verbose
penciled a loved metaphor & said flatly it go
even thanked lucky stars whenever you missed
a deep midnight thought had saved from despair   grateful for
wrenching of a tender phrase any daring page's crumpled horn

3

& so will the debt endure forever?
how is it your image of a mantelpiece
means more than any have managed in all these years?
were the glass figures ocelots or leopards?
they've remained a menagerie of burnished words

though reading that poem after marriage & degrees
would fail to find any sleekness there
feared admit it had been a mere period piece
its diction that seemed so modern in tone

just imitative & yet had driven me on

even the mirror & flame of its memory
shine finer than any I've cast
or that simple but subtle living-room scene
though perhaps no setting you even composed
is yet the sum of all I have deeply owed

in dreams have given back an aura only
half the glow that printed fireplace gave
can merely return as reflection has forever since
on critics you quoted on your inspiring demurs
this ember lit from that matchless verse

Carroll Black: Author of *Stephen Hero*

had come to Lamar Tech from Orange
a city just inside the Texas line
that invisible border through bayous
stretching beyond into Cajun wilds

his hometown reached by a highway lifted
up & over the Neches River
tankers below heading out for the Gulf
or inland to port as they floated beneath

that "rainbow" bridge with its black gold view
to scummy reeds   at night the soaring flames
burning off gas   nothing close to his prose
his retouched portraits of Dedalus or Bloom

for even as a freshman his one ambition
to write another *Ulysses*
how he'd found the classics   reared in swamps
the biggest mystery of that mystical year

mother swore his underwear trimmed with lace
the Ds he made in German bothered much more
couldn't equate his Buck Mulligan manner with
the grades he pulled   on clarinet seated last chair

but from here he comes in clear   waiting for class
leaning in the hall   in that same black rayon suit
a silk white shirt   re-reading *Dubliners* or *Leaves of Grass*
nearest thing to Joyce's protagonist the college knew

introduced Faulkner & the latest MJQ
loaned the *Fontessa* album said Listen to
their Harlequin piece It's the greatest hit
The Commedia dell' Arte through a jazz quartet!

Hear those four Blacks in tails with their delicate touch
reviving the Italian Renaissance in bluesy tones
heard it echoed off walls of neighboring homes
where crews half-slept till the graveyard shift

spinning the record past two a.m.
we repeated how dull those schoolmates were
applied to each all that author had meant
so certain had awakened at Finnegan's words

to a tower overlooked the pains of love
a jetty built by the winds of our wits
books piled for the crossing to Paris
exile   definition   refinement   horse piss!

since then have been   not there   but abroad
& it just ain't so   homesick   confused
tortured by doubt   the natives intimidating
their chants of hands-off politics

no sensitive lines came easy or tough
just a picture of that Liberal Arts hall
superimposed while riding crushed in a bus
straining to catch at the quick foreign phrase

wondering where he was   how the novel progressed
thought of Pierre Menard rewriting Cervantes
curious if Carroll had done it to "The Dead"
as for me still continued to imitate Yeats

haunted still by his talk of those Irish greats
still warmed by memories of a *Portrait*'s first page
till remembrance went cold as baby tuckoo's bed sheet
hopeless as that blind block of North Richmond Street

yet revisited & believed in those Beaumont scenes
of him lounging in the hall with its lighting dim
off discolored walls & unbuffed floors
the books in his hands held mostly for looks

but still let in by him as if through a door
to the wonder of this   a place to fit
a form to fill   boiling of crude down to a fuel
the cleansing ethyl for an art to steer

gaining for one raised on bayou or marsh
faith in the refinery as an image can mean
though what he opened stayed closed to him
with his dreams of novels unsoiled by the near

now feeling it more deeply than ever   the failure
of this poem he deserves in return
can hope at least for this fellow who led the way
that cliché may follow   'tis better to give than etcetera

Footwear News

This is a poem of the smell of a place,
a shoe & boot repair to be exact.
Last night outside Dawson, Texas,
none of the 84 survived, all was wreckage.

Here then is how a cobbler who's half the time
with half a beard, who's yet to attend
any church but customers' aches & complaints,
who long ago stopped up to his business' sacred scent,

put it in this poem's mind to dry that sinus, bring it
back again. Peter Marshall's life on film: I see him,
just after a night-school class in French,
throwing down the text, almost stepping off a cliff

when he's saved by a presence trips him near the edge.
Movies moved me then, still can if camera pan up
in the face of a feeling these strips of leather leave me
with, but things themselves sooner take me there.

And now I watch & want to weep as he works my shoe
down onto an upright metal sole, pulls a nail
from the side of his mouth, pounds it into the heel,
five more & the wobble's healed.

I see the machine he sews it on, a simple tool
does a job of stitching so fast & sure
I'd all but forgotten what the mind can do,
forgot the better walk we save time for–

sniff the ether of his quick-drying glue, not
to take a "trip" as high schoolers do, but just
to have the odor fixed of how cement is applied to the
welt, German for world, & our only matter now,

for though planes fall, the hike's still on,
this is a poem, & those are gone
beyond the word's repair, spilt milk
in the farmer's tragic phrase—& yet

this music in my mind's a paste to give a shine
to the scuffed & dried, the cracked &
weather-worn, buffs itself into feeling song
can sing back in—movement on their own,

for since the subject's seldom a man, with in his
hand a hammer, ever the bitter ash wind will lift
& scatter, I let him lead me by the open nose
in & around this, his aromatic, paradisal shop,

with its heavy-duty thread passing into eyes,
its scraps of tan cowhide, black neolite under foot,
beveled arches ready at hand, to hold up failing touch,
joyful journeys upon his shelf, inside a *Cat's Paw* box.

A Drop-Out Photo of December '69

To the east side of each stand of trees
a thin length of snow continues to
cling, each trunk made more
distinct, ornamented by
the ermine cold.

The early sun,
distorted in shimmering through
this freezing air,
takes on a blinding brightness
would deny the time of year.

And now o so slowly arrive
light & falling flakes enough to
dress fully these dark & barren
days, when the mind can come only
to conclusions too violent to bear.

Before the Fire

The kindling stacked, the shavings set,
a first fire in this new home grate
blazes up in his sparkling eyes,
as I stoke with fears, build worries

out of what if, and if, then when
I'll have to move the family again,
feeling how a boy's mind yearns
to make the signals out, even if it burns.

Distant now, he stirs embers with a stick,
I with thoughts of living in the thick
of things, a colleague fired, the threat
conveyed as even here this fireplace heat.

A knight, he draws forth his flaming sword,
lifts it to the blackened flue, one bright guard
against the dark. I'm wondering who comes next,
nearer now on the enemies' list, at every rumor vexed.

Staring awed into the open hearth, he spots
a blue gas streaming out. I'm remembering Watts,
as he proclaims, it's dragon's breath, then asks
what are those, those red-looking bricks,

jabbing at the glowing rectangular hunks
of vibrant fiber, uncovering charred chunks,
smoked, he declares, like a ribbed eraser
he cleaned at school. I reach for a chaser,

recall how easy a man's rubbed out,
his job done away with, days filled with doubt.

Cheeks flushed as coals, and so at home,
the lookout bends closer, spies a comb,

white ash of a dying brand like bees-
wax, says others run with honey, though these
I can't make out, want, need to, even more to accept
bitter with sweet, a son's wonder, with words unkept.

Shoe-Dog Rimes

1: *waiting*

hating how slow the hours go
then see the spastic in greater slow-
motion jerk to a chair slightly drool
sit down too hard before the fitting stool

with one thin foot one so much big-
ger & each ankle skinny as a possum's leg
one shoe gaping while the other cramps
yet happy that among such stylish pumps

this pair of ugly oxfords & the only offer
pains her less than her old clodhoppers
broken-down ties she's dragged in mud & dust
through heat of the shoe-dog's dragging August

2: *testimonial*

son you surprise me bending there
when another salesman down the street
was flat afraid to wait on me
told me this here artificial limb

felt to him like a dead man's foot
said to touch it give him the willies
Lord this hollow plastic stump
most wonderful thing ever come along

after being down for months
losing my own when the toes gangrened

suddenly I could rise & go like in the Bible
when the healed took up his couch & walked

3: *mates*

the farmer's wife measures a full eleven
"thank heaven you all still carry my number"
says so even at two dollars extra above size ten
"she never finds nothing to fit at these summer

sales"   mentions how Medicare failed to pay
when a heifer had tromped the living day-
lights out of him   hearing it again she shudders
"all he could see in his face was udders"

"& hooves honey hooves kept stomping down
& after I'd been there looking in on her fail-
ing calf   always happens helping someone else"
"his brain surgeon removed a bone this big around"

"here where the scar's healed over the hair's
come back   but I ain't gone in that pasture since
if you need black too just be sure don't nothing pinch
we won't be getting into town now for half a year"

"feels fine dear   at dawn we walk out a good five
miles & slowly now he's gaining back his gait"
"hell I damned near died   lucky to be alive
go on mother I'll buy you both pair   let's celebrate"

4: *corn*

a dance the Indians did
a prayer said for the staple they ate

124

cereal of a civilization
winged its way from the Andes

to Tamaulipas & Bat Cave
ground   on the cob   or popped
for a shoot 'em up Lash Larue picture show
when the aroma reached from the ticket booth

made one's mouth to water
standing in line for those buttered puffs
like yellowed clouds   such a poor answer
to their chants for rain

in moving so much the Lipan Apache
forgot what made the tassels grow
had to ask the white man how to plant
the reason it comes on toes is this:

no right foot-leather relationship
squeezing of feet into plastic slippers
dreaming for our belittled lives
a Cinderella fairyland size

a crippling fit will win the Prince
yet cultivates only inflammation
in the coolest air-conditioning
forms beads of burning sweat on

brows furrowed as Caddo fields
their best ears hung in well-smoked homes
in case the crop should fail
the last seed perish

kernels of black orange red
strung for decoration
shucks platted & woven for dolls
in Latin nations taking in Spanish

an animal or a flower name
in Cuba known as a rose
in Chile a goat with sugar coating
in Mexico termed a pigeon-dove

but this is a needless human growth
its seed sprouts a numbing at the root
produces just irritation
no hybrid this corn is rather

hubris bred
raised from seeking
the shorter the smaller
a choice that grows but briar & thorn

5: *cuboid*

the Cuboid Kid writes again
rides shotgun goes orthopedic guard
against false or awkward starts
that burning sensation   will gladly explain

arches ma'am you've four in all
transverse & metatarsal
inner & outer longitudinal
& this little pad we call

a cuboid holds them up like
banks or trains

well as the west bridge spans
comes thin thick narrow wide

same as your body of water
moves with the bones & leather
to catch you that bus or husband
good for the get-away from a stuck-up man

will save from running over
new & expensive browns or blues
the swollen way a channel does
or any creek dammed by beaver

son are you kidding me?
no ma'am never a bit
not the Cuboid Kid
I'd sooner saddle me than be

strapped with any sin of omission
would rather take a lower commission
than rob a customer of how to stand
when it seems she simply can't

would lend support for when it counts
break up any heist of a shopper's relief
having taken no oath of an unfitting belief
in chicken-little skies falling all around

the way remember when Wells Fargo
saw their bargain shares begin to go
down daily on the stock exchange?
this'll keep you vault safe from ambulant pain

Rio Grande

came never intending to leech off friends
but stayed for a week then half a year
cannot remember how or who invited
only where & why each yet stands clear
had slept here on a daybed in between
a space heater & the back porch screen
with its plastic sheet flapping all night long
from the autumn & then the winter wind
one side freezing & the other done
merely existing at 2300 Rio Grand'
my realer romantic self still in Chile
from where in September had just returned
there but a month though it seemed as if
had never left just worked at Dacy's to earn
for a trip would rejoin those divided selves
ready once more to quit this city
where in years to come across 23rd
would watch our Elisa first *tendu*
bend & stretch at that wooden bar
lifting rising toward the balletic art
an inconceivable gift María would give
but then unknown as also Estevan's day
when he & afterwards President Lamar
had created the schools laid out the roads
would pave the way for her training here
her slowly preparing for pains on pointe
knew only to toss & turn from hot to cold
on that mattress a thrall to such paradox
gripped by fears of how when or even if
by an icy lust smoldered deep within
for one with whom it wasn't meant

yet wondrously drawn to hurry back
through all that wrong to find at last
the rightness of a ballerina born of her
whose *pas de chats* to piano strains
would bring her close as half a block
at ABT her classes first with Joanie
then once the studio moved to one on 5th
with Lisa Smith feather light as Juliet
& later still at Ballet Austin on Guadalupe
the renovated station of Hose Company No. 6
studying with Miss León & Mrs. Loomis
never guessed nor half surmised
the wars they fought with Santa Anna
Lipan Apache Karankaway the Comanche
the taxes levied & their soles replaced
would lead to a daughter's graceful steps
ignorant then of Estevan's love repressed
his journey ending on a procrustean bed
his sacrifice unknown for all it was worth
had only crossed this river-street back & forth
sweating the German & government tests
mostly concerned Verónica wouldn't care
had abandoned place & people all for her
felt even as Lamar though hardly aware
when Mirabeau invaded Doña Carlota's land
marched to Monterrey from the Rio Grand'
to save that nation from its "erring mind"
by a sense of duty torn & pulled both ways
by the one he'd lost with his valiant sword
"But wo is me / Between us roars a gloomy stream"
while Villagrá captain-poet with Oñate's men
had paddled against its fateful current
trekked sands no Christian foot had ever trod
through briars & nets of stinging twigs

lashed at eyes & ripped at armorless legs
their bare swollen feet at the mercy of
the scabrous rocks & high hot dunes
more than fifty days marching on & on
for seven straight in a drenching rain
at the end of a final four without a drop
in their haste the horses would overdrink
with their flanks filled dying "satisfied"
blinded by dagger sun & piñon lance
some waded out too far then swept away
by a wealth of waters could not believe
Oñate's men spread out along its banks
like bloated toads or tavern drunks
all this river to them not nearly enough
to slake their parched & voiceless throats
then shown at El Paso a convenient ford
by those barbarians with crude instincts
hunting & fishing & living off roots
never breaking earth or planting seeds
unconcerned grand cities grew in far León
ignored the stir of palace or highest court
nor had they ever to face red tape
impediments to Oñate's moving ahead
delayed for months by jealous hatred
uncouth contented unsuspicious brutes
leading them across at the very point
where border guards would stop the car
on coming back from shopping in Júarez
with a black sheep cousin & his Chicana wife
María still breast-feeding Darío then
the officer stooping to search inside
to ask "Is everyone here a U.S. citizen?"
she a registered alien answered Chilean
when the trouble & rude treatment all began

her card left in Hobbs she could not come in
she & the baby must remain on that other side
"But wo is me / Between us roars a gloomy stream"
phoned to friends told them just break in
ransack the house & find that Green Card
the one with her picture she detested so
whose magic numbers could divide Red Seas
would let them pass over & bring them back
the two kept there & by more than water
so cruelly cut off by the indifferent law
while passage to Beauty's Santiago home
enabled by those who roomed on this street
its Spanish name a link to her long thin land
its blocks strolled with friends or all alone
on visits to Gilliam's Brick Row shelves
at 1913 but on the corner somehow of 21st
his Book Shop with its Hardy & Howells
those first 1st editions had bought & read
a volume of Spenser introduced by Yeats
William Dean's novel *The Shadow of a Dream*
like the one fell on Estevan ever & again
along the way lost all but *Moments of Vision*
never a feeling those too were there & then
writing on the Hardy end sheet "Austin '61"
when I'd rib correct proper & superior Jon
with his size thirteens & the yellowed leaves
rained down & stuck to heels from misted walks
shrill grackles whistling in bare-limbed trees
their wet black branches darkening against
the gray-orange-pink of autumn's sunset sky
gave hope even here a poem might come to life
in years before those nights on Hickeys' porch
when Mary Jane tired of seeing a poet-type
asleep out there or scribbling in her kitchen

or ironing a dress shirt for work each morning
she cooking Dave's breakfast & chatting a bit
to be civil while thinking Why doesn't he leave?
but stayed on through fall '65 into winter '66
a nuisance to them though would always pay
yet how could 25 dollars ever cover the sight
of being there whenever they returned at night
passed through that "bedroom" to enter their own
had at least used the toilet & shower at Lonn's
his garage apartment back of their big two-storey
next door to Leslie who would loan her phone
a bother to all but still each putting up with
the savings made & the mooning over love
in the meantime butt of their Elephant jokes
once gone appropriated the Spiller & Baugh
those expensive hardback literary histories
could feel no rancor to lose such books
since not even those would ever repay
the inconvenience of such a worn-out stay
just wishing this perhaps may compensate
if those times with all their impositions
their kindnesses & "moments of vision"
should bring at least a painful pleasure
beyond any imbursement of a costlier kind
by allowing these sketches of former days
to make small return for all they gave
for theirs as worthy if written up right
as the lives & letters in that reference set
Hickey in cowboy boots & blue-jean pants
all he would wear unless his Stetson
as in between polishing his paragraphs
he would lift his bare mole-ridden back
to catch in a heave his second breath
like his hero Fitzgerald unable to spell

signed up for a course to get some help
his name noticed on that remedial roll
by the Dean took away his assistantship
then at the Student Union holding forth
on the latest theories linguistic or fictive
holing up at that house on Rio Grande
seated day & night in his book-lined study
taking a deep drag a swig from his *Pepsi*
shut off by closing those sliding doors
to correct & type up his Texas stories
of buttering tortillas or hunting quail
the authentic life & death of Smiley Logan
who at 12 hit Odessa's National Bank
at 25 by a truck load of underfed steers
his best of a TV newsman in San Antone
a Jewish ambulance chaser met his match
in the Mexican mother of George Guzmán
who viewed his slow dying filmed & shown
unflinching in the face of a car wreck's jaws
of her own son she saw there pinned inside
for her the newsman's re-run a liturgical song
Garland Marlinberg a priest had offered it up
such scenes Hickey meant for the magazines
The New Yorker   Harper's   The Atlantic
looked ever East for the acceptance signs
gave it all up when they hadn't arrived
his tale of a nude rancher dies in his tub
McMurtry lists in his *In a Narrow Grave*
but merits a place on this roll call more
for bringing them out as Estevan before
lines & pages of native or immigrant alike
edited for *Riata* & given welcome at home
where authors & artists all gathered to meet
came in a steady stream to this river-street

prose & pigment talk overflowing the rooms
their canvases hung where Mary Jane served
as gracious host to the unwashed anarchists
Gilbert Shelton showing off his latest t-shirt
featured Wonder Wart Hog's bristling snout
known too for drawing that satirical Ranger
a stunted Hairy with long holstered six-guns
such figures created for his serial cartoons
their comments made in social & political fun
or with Hairy pictured on that *Ranger* cover
peering up at a Mona Lisa bears his ugly mug
in its caption spouting to the museum guard
he didn't know nothin' 'bout no *modren* art
but by god he knew he liked what he saw
& Jaxson's underground *Rag* the nation's first
was it he who drew that so classic strip
of Maddox' finger-lickin' good fried chicken
of that owner wielding his racist lumber
whose attitude toward his Negro cook
gets radically adjusted by Super Good
but not before the hero's battered & bruised
by Lester's axe-handle answer to protest
when a light bulb goes on over Super's head
he'll take a black indelible ink & dye the bigot
& so many others like Beeson & Osborn
Harold writing "A Matter of Possession"
in a room rented together summer of '63
around the block from the Robert E. Lee
from a bar Mort would frequent regularly
after practice walking on 21st past Littlefield
its Coppini web-footed horses & sudsy fountain
for a *Lone Star* longneck & a large sour pickle
home by the watered lawns of frail landladies
tough customers when it came time to collect

ran musty boarding houses on the up & up
served creamed cauliflower & plenty of spuds
but couldn't hold out against a push for space
another house & street forever displaced
another memoried address has given way
yet won't let go though there's not a trace
as when Sugar & Turpin are both released
just when Clarence's turn has come at last
to claim as throne their jail cell's only chair
but with neither to see him its meaning lost
when he rips off the legs & kicks in the seat
laughing burns them all in hysterical defeat
& though to most it won't matter a bit
leveled will hold to their image the more
a character in Carolyn's "Ancient History"
her early story from *Riata* spring of '64
crazy old Miss Agnes Doyle to a prissy girl
hell no she don't have no telephone
& all you need's a good switchin'
declares "of the two kinds of not knowing
not knowing where you've been is worse"
Hickey printing others by Branda & Giles
not then Jim's tale of Whitman's "August Day"
came later with its "landscape of Spanish-brick
fountains and statuary ranging from lifeless"
to "the bloody mangled bodies in his wake"
rather poems then by Wally Stopher the 3rd
& by Tom Whitbread would sit one night
on the edge of that daybed there out back
with a party at the Hickeys' roaring inside
had not then given it up spoke under the effects
of what it might have been too sleepy to catch
most likely of the trains he so truly loves
from *Triad*'s third number can hear his lines

taking to task a *Harper's* "reporter/distorter"
of these streets & the *Texas Eagle's* diner car
Wally last seen bound east on a campus shuttle
snaggletoothed & needing the price of a string
said without a guitar it kept him from singing
wondered without his teeth had his talent gone
or with less to begin with had been better off
just picking up lines from all these others
& "for a song" as laureate Barney has sung
in these "certain discoverable neighborhoods"
here on Estevan's river & numbered streets
from Hickey's contributors like Mueller Lewis
whose haunting "Homespun Idyll" forever weaves
how Buddo turns from spider to a victim trapped
in the triumph of his own subtle sabotage web
or from Eldon who rediscovered Christina Stead
then caught up for ten years in revising the facts
for *The Handbook of Texas* set his novel aside
to verify names of odd townships now owed to him
Fono bringing over "Circus" by Frigyes Karinthy
after escape from his Hungary invaded by tanks
on Rio Grande received & accepted without exception
& later on 12th at Hickey's gallery naturally named
after "Papa's" story "A Clean Well-Lighted Place"
Dave like a selfless Estevan promoting their work
till he up & left it all for old New York
predictably losing to that tempting Big Apple
his lovely Eve from Midland-Odessa
with her deep accent forever distinctive
its desert sweetness so clear & clean
not oil slick as her Permian Basin
but welling up as if artesian
rich in its unassuming ingenuous ring
looked back from another hot business trip

an exhibit in Chicago Nashville or Omaha
to lose her among the lonely office halls
watched as his Eurydice half disappeared
into a known attorney's awaiting arms
saw his own employment evaporate too
as an agent then for the pop-art rage
that famous quote his parting shot
at the boss had gone & double-crossed
him & all of his painter friends
"the ship abandoned a sinking rat"
while Estevan never left except for them
to carry their case to congressional sessions
gave up those plans for erecting his home
putting up Mary Holley & hearing her voice
digging their garden to her strummed guitar
"I entered upon the busy stage of life
with ideas which had they been true
would have made this Earth a paradise
dreams of youth unpoisoned by ambition
my angel Mother kind hearted father
my first standards of human nature
wealth was not the incentive led me here
Ambition kindled its fires in my breast
but the flame was a mild and gentle one
consisting more of the wish to build up
the others' fortunes and happiness
asylum for sufferers from selfish avarice
the mania for speculation
and you my friend
how shall I ever thank you enough
for venturing into this wilderness
how express the happiness
of the ten days visit
Gardens and rosy bowers

and ever verdant groves
music books and intellectual amusements
can all be ours
Millions could not buy them
but the right disposition with competence
insure them"
his words intended for María too
spoken as well of whoever endured
a shameless poet the way Lonn did
as days turned into weeks & months
of shaving & bathing & listening to
his recording of a Prokofieff ballet
Cinderella foretelling Elisa's *plié*
chiming a warning it was time to go
his classical collection surprising so
even more his mind on hearing his drawl
his by far the deepest guttural
a snorting infectious high-pitched laugh
no idle claim of "nowhere but Texas"
consumed by the case bock *Shiner* beer
knew state politics Schulenberg to Freer
could speak to the meaning of a post-oak fence
Virginia worm   zig-zag   split-rail   stake & rider
each "impervious to cattle hogs or high winds"
"a more handsome ornament than the chain-link"
suddenly his booming voice turned sentimental
as he'd plead with Leslie to go for a pitcher
down at Scholz Garten before they'd close
when her text of *Child Psych* fell to the floor
then squeezed as a threesome in his VW Bug
was she first mentioned the book by Griffith
her ex-teacher on a Dickinson under duress
its "Long Shadow" cast for all these years
her own too who saw to it others got through

lent moral support before that call to Chile
& afterwards when it came to a choice
set her love life aside to listen & serve
a Sacajawea who guided safely across
yet what solace can these memories be
a re-run of collisions have mostly outlived
of survivors changed from young & cocky
so certain our plans would all work out
in some ways turned out for the better
if for the worse can retracing a stream
reverse where waters ran out of control
in a blind moment dragged so quickly down
with the rudder gone why recover an oar
in remembrance can a river ever hope to renew
in holding to it won't it just grow stagnant
no answers to show only this lifted footage
this spring tide of a gratitude flows on & on

María's Bath

locking herself in there she left us
panting here outside this door
let kids pets & hubby know
in no uncertain terms
was not to be disturbed

with her beyond our sight & touch
are feeling low & utterly lost
stand or pace about & listen hard
for sounds of water run or poured
for the dead bolt shot to life

hear it & sniff her aroma emerge
renewed by luffa after all her chores
soaked & sponged by lavender soap
rinsed off & now more lovely & soft
rubbing her again all whine & purr

*   *   *

though applied & smoothed the caulk
more than once from its smelly tubes
each with a guarantee the job would last
& touched up twice the plastic tiles
first with a yellow paint she simply hates
& then with something called "rustoleum"
the label stated would stop or money back
already the ugly stains have started again
at the edge of this unsightly mildewed tub
where half-submerged she stretched herself
with her brown eyes fully closed upon

her modest pair of lily pads
this rent house room now misses so
having to fall back on its glaring fixtures
its garish color none she would ever have
the one the landlord said to leave alone
told her rudely just to let it be
though this recalls such dreams of her
coming here with her book to read
with her apple pared to eat
to add more water hot or cold
with her little wondrous toes

& yet on revisiting the scene
it only reveals
her Chilean author's wet memoir
on the rim her bitten core
rusting with all the rest of it
no other sign
not another left to find
even the ring washed down the drain
& with the mirror now unfogged
stare vacantly at a scrawny Texan neck
instead of catching the hoped-for glimpse
just the reflection of all her loveliness
set against this dingy enamel
yet even to know she bathed in here
puts such shabbiness head & shoulders above
the most luxurious sunken brand
turns this cheap paint job into
a pure primeval pond
viewed as through a clearing in
creation's mist
regains this room's lost innocence
dresses it in the freshest fruit & shade

recovering as if by a page leafed through
by soft warm ungrasping fingers
the watermarked promise
of an unending garden plot
nor would ever see it changed

María's Mandolin

rests inside its orange-lined case
with its hollow form unembraced
its neck not held nor danced upon
its strings untuned & uncaressed
can lift no song nor lilt a phrase

nor can it leave the closet yet
stored beneath the sheets & spreads
the quilts & blankets for another year
shut away with children's winter wear
against a season they're grown & gone

no time she says no time to play
must sweep & wash & bake & sew
how can I hope to practice now
come home you want your supper on
cook or concertize I can't do both

& so must long & listen to Prokofiev
the score for Romeo & his Juliet
with its contradanse for mandolins
to hear her fingers & to linger on
each tone she'll give upon that day

when chords return the words & notes
of her mamita's Chilean voice
can make no sound upon its own
must await for María to set it free
from death's own closet & leather case

though shelved beyond her reach
even now can feel it ring within
its tremolos recounting all the nights
she's held this head & kissed the frets
till her music's filled all emptiness

María's Menagerie

one by one her brood has come
her Bremen band of musicians
until their invasion has over-

whelmed this house & yard
only the donkey
has yet to arrive

with his pitiful song
his braying at sunset
his heehaw at dawn

she still impatient
for the smell of his sweat
of his fresh green cakes

from mash & hay
those already here
came frisky & young

unlike the bunch
in the Grimm brothers' tale
whose useful days

had come to an end
their owners bent
on drowning cooking or doing them in

would make a meal
of those had served
cut back on costs of keeping them fed

of her own
only the layers have
paid their way

the Siamese cat
has been declawed
to save the upholstery on the sofa bed

though surgery came too late
for in a scampering & jumping fit
had dug a scratch

in her antique dresser
her hand still bearing a scar
from that treacherous adorable pet

the one on her wrist above her thumb
when it wanted down
& growled against

another lipstick kiss on its forehead fur
but has never forgotten & still regrets
the pain she made her kitten feel

with bloody paws wrapped
taped like a challenger's fists
just before some title match

for days till the drug wore off
her Mushto looking punchy
with groggy eyes & feinting moves

her dog an ugly worthless mutt
overweight with its legs too short

too dumb to bark at would-be thieves

good for nothing but fleas
& to lie on flowers she's nursed along
to suck the eggs of her exotic hen

Guacolda with her big green feet
lays shells of a matching tint
a cross between a Spanish breed

& a Chilean fowl Araucanian
as her namesake in
Ercilla's epic poem

Lautaro's beloved spouse
whose dream of his tragic death
at the hands of troops

Villagrán would lead
came true as almost in Chaucer
his Chauntecleer's

like him her Chester a mock heroic
cocky in his spurs & crenellated comb
let the whole block know how he was here

with a morning crow nearly woke the dead
so irritated one guy down the street
threw bottles & stones at first

but then from his own backyard
before the kids were off to school
aimed a pump or pellet gun

at his puffed & colorful breast
took the wind right out of him
finishing forever his wing-dipping dance

raccoon & possum sneaking in
to snack on Dottie & La salvaje
her other hens

after which Guacolda
before the sun has set
will cluck outside the door

fly up & peck
at the kitchen window
no more chicken coop for her

since then will roost in the den
& was welcomed in as if this home
were Ma Kettle's in *The Egg and I*

recalls how Gala would always swear
with too much love for the animal kingdom
there's little left for humankind

it's mostly just that all are jealous
husband son & daughter of affection showered
on any brute from mongrel to her nasty cat

yet know she still has more than enough
to spread around deserved or not
though none for toads snakes or a certain neighbor

María's Photograph

stranded on that proverbial desert isle
if not allowed herself
the choice would be her photograph
not one from the album stored within
but any of the few untorn in two
& tossed away o how she hates them all!

just as much as I so covet each
like this color print I'm gazing upon
has kept her with her hair cut short
though in the beach wind's blown enough
to allow far inland this summoning up
of her breathing deeply of its salty air

with behind her head the water blue
the sky of lighter & darker shades
white splashes of cloud to either side
& between them she seems a mermaid
yet it's never a fable whenever she's near
though even then it's so unreal

having her close night after night
even more to hold her years away
in this simple sleeveless top
with throat & shoulders bare
in October there at Corpus
whose Gulf coast can't compare

with Chile's brilliant stretch of sea
where a week before that wedding day
her skin took on such a radiant tan

grew almost weak with wanting her
after she'd gone with Gala & was left to mope
never guessing she'd return even lovelier yet

& while there is little here to recommend
with these lukewarm waves just lazing in
crumbling sand castles too harsh to touch
even so this Texas beach has held her in
its most becoming light
has done its best to measure up

as if it somehow knew
it had to compete was up against
her vast & rich Pacific
whose tides take in such climates
reach to such cultures continents away
as these poor shores can only dream

could hardly hope to fathom
her Basque Arabic & Sephardic strands
but thank this native breeze & inclement sun
for their lesser glow they lend her still
brings back that trembling all over again
when on that day she answered *sí* I will

María's Tapestry

before her consent to my insistent plea

& contrary to the uniformed official who
at the swearing-in declared on February 2
this date you enter the US of A remember
is the most important in all of your life
meaning to say she had only married me
to escape the poverty of a dumb Spanish way

had never thought to leave her long thin land
but chose like the biblical Moabite Ruth
to take this people & place as her own
though that was prior to meeting the two
for once she heard the murder of words
in English & in her warm native tongue
knew our deep need for spray-net & rouge
& sweated from hundred-degree heat in the shade

her picture of La Chimba now hangs on the wall
grew clearer in spite of its distance & days
from that Chilean valley of her summers & youth
till not to carry such a paradise about
cooped up alone in her homeless head
country to country & house to rented house
she came in Illinois to sew & piece out
her grandfather's parcel near the seaport La Serena
with colored yarn & some remnants of cloth
worked on a burlap backing tacked to a rod

its stream with flowers & white picket fence
its arbor with grapes grown luscious with dust

its garden with corn rows carrots & beets
its bees buzzing about their half-oval hive
its trees with paisley patches for leaves
brown print mountains blue sheeting with birds
the washing on lines the primitive-sized ducks
embroidered green vines all climbing the walls

made it to keep from doing the same
on moving to New Mexico or South Carolina
living in an apartment where a couple next door
spent half the nights cursing & crying
the husband slapping & pounding the wife
she weeping then flinging a book or a shoe
would thud where this crewelwork suspended
memories had traveled far from their source

further from an Eden have tried to replace
to match with tarantulas horned-frogs & snakes
nothing to blend with her worsted wool
cuttings from Darío's corduroys Elisa's playsuits
remnants with which an alien graced this fallen earth
tempted to by a Texan's foul-weather love

Petri in Texas: 1851-1857

after a text by W.W. Newcomb

a pencil sketch marks the choice
for some a loss of higher art
to Lipan squaws

his on mule back   not even sidesaddle
their bowed legs bare
& straddling   one   with an el-

bow bent   propped on a mare
stretches out & lounges along
her wingless mount

her left knee crooked
her leg held doubled   the foot
unlady-like up & level with

the horse's rump
to capture it would take the trail
away from Apollo's sacred hill

chose between the signpost hands
digits pointing to opposing roads:
Parnassus or   the wilderness

told his picture tale on a notebook page
his doodling the size of an index card
a 3 x 5 reply to muses in the background

faint figures sitting around
taking the fountained waters
up above a choking cloud

a dust raised
by the hooves of
his plodding Texas Pegasus

carries him away
to Fredericksburg
far from spirits had first in-

spired this student Dresden-
schooled his Nazarene
teacher a mystic recluse

could have assured him the prize or tenure
would have lifted him to the academic
to the allegorical portraiture

with its clear theatrical gaze
its full lines & features   its foot-high bust
of a nude young Dionysus

angels hovering open-mouthed
traded their caroling for
two log cabins

a farm on the Pedernales
river his fever drowned him in
the drawing left of where they lived

a rough & ready home in frontier space
& on the sheet floating sideways

a settler's bearded profile

a woman's classic look beside
a red-tongued dog
a baroque coyote

the sky of weird water-colored smears
kaleidoscopic shades
done in his lap or on some stump

in no studio with fleshly models
here his only suggestive touch
the rustic midnight episode

of a pioneer in wide-brimmed hat
attacks with an axe in hand
a bull snake after the eggs

his wife in see-through cotton gown
at the lighted henhouse door
hesitating in fear

this rather than a Virgin & child
positioned at the triangular center
of his earlier nativity scene

arched in an alcove
of divinity & love
the husband & cattle about her

the heavenly host gathered above
while here his native event appears
on paper brown as a grocery bag

faded by unmerciful sun
& not to waste his scarce supplies
the artist has crammed in miniature

a horse-backed man
with thick surrounding woods
hinted at by three trees overlapping

their limbs a rugged arbor
formed to the rider's sides
he hatted & in his slicker

slightly bent to miss the twigs
emerging out of or into
never more

than met the eye
such sights & weather as
only he perhaps would

have ever set down
nor can any now
nor any ever again

the unwashed drawn with a
cleanness puts to shame
his "Madonna of roses" done

with a posed embrace
of her too-mature stark-
naked cherub boy

her flowing robes & sensuous toes
no match for the Plains mother's plainness

not combed & re-combed tresses but windblown

no flowers wound in coiffured strands
but a sleeveless *huipil* of practical cut
her lips at rest on the papoose head

her own bowed low
the mule stopped
or moving slow

humble or humiliated
proud or dispossessed
their eyes saying more

than we'd wish to know
his years here short yet long on art
spent them poring over

what changing times
would soon be dis-
posing of

elsewhere other views
maybe of the artist himself
flailing grain in

suspenders
in his striped pants &
flannel shirt

a husband trudging through winter mud
piggybacking his bonneted bride
hogs dozing in sun   chickens   dogs

warriors with eyebrows plucked
braided queues dragged in dirt
a buckskinned girl with a melon rind

his delicate sway between
the primitive &
a training European

the chalk line
from Dresden to
Fredericksburg

has tied the two in a drawing
of an inadvertent
tightrope act

a man balanced
on a longhorn's nose
a glimpse of Friedrich's equilibrium

in the agile reel
of a tipsy grenadier
toasting an antlered deer

the genius of his German pen
discovered only in his throwing in
with women milking

Comanches with hands & faces
painted blue   their lances fringed
one Penateka sucking on a fifth

stuck in the pocket
of a bluecoat who
sits there unawares

at a big powwow
for pushing them back
& in his taking sides

with those could ill afford
nor would they have thought
to pay his meager fees

much less to enter a gallery
to see themselves bigger alive than
even they would have ever believed

busy making progress
breaking treaties   eating jowls
slopping pigs   in Parnassian style

The Historian Has Lost His Chair

the one endowed
for half-a-million
alleged to have left
our state & nation

a week before the
president had said he
could she the Regents'
lame-duck that's who

have read in his work
on the Driskill Hotel
like best the part on
Ben the bartender

checked out from the
library a book per day
his way to learn
what plan to suggest

to the architect
hot after a bid
whether the politician
should wager a bet

mixing at the Headliners Club
drinks for the professoriate
then drying shot glasses
as those tenured all sat

their talk a swirl
of blue Cuban smoke

for this chair I'm fixing
María only paid a dollar
her garage-sale bargain
though in need of repairs

& after half a day
there's still no end
to these plastic strips
at two-&-a-quarter apiece

weave first these by-
products of Arabian oil
then tighten each screw
on the aluminum frame

make believe
it's bamboo or cane
& I'm a craftsman
in complete disguise

squatting on Elisa's
dollhouse seat
lends me leverage
a hold on how

half the world
has sat cross-legged
cooler on floors
than sweat up a storm

on a vinyl or a
Herculon couch

now watch a caterpillar
hunching this slab
a fuzzy brown ripple
I turn to a smear

as the sole of my sandal
goes sliding with ease
on its guts went green
from mulberry leaves

over those he & friends
all gathered to pitch
their see-through tents
each twitching in gauze

enwrapped our trees
as though with angel hair
bought the latest sprays
burned the lower limbs

nothing doing the trick
till all over town
they suddenly quit
moved on to mate or metamorphose

this stain well on its way
when it got rubbed out
by a belated revenge
since every twig stripped

is shooting green flames
as if after summer comes spring

o once this furniture
for the lawn's renewed
I'll sit outside
in a coat of repellent

& gaze while the sky
of our Austin night
flowers & flickers
as with cured Havanas

will dream of promotion
to a high funded chair
or of tending in Texas
an historical bar

where ahead of the rest
I'll arrive in a flash
to understand hallways
or a passage of law

where taking off early
or to get away late
won't mean they'll jerk
your seat out from under

nor come down hard
after you've had your fill
& you're headed on out
to try & discover

*a way to love
or transfigure*

John Lang Sinclair: Class Poet

viewed by millions on network TV
how many Longhorn fans
giving their Hook 'em signs
with index & little fingers
have leaped to their feet
in stadium or stands
to resound his words throughout the land
inspired by Prather's paraphrase
of Robert E. Lee
John Lang penning his lines
on Bosch's now-browned laundry paper
in nineteen three
after Lewis had locked him
in room 305 of old "B" Hall
& his friends would keep him there
forcing him to finish the jest
in time for Varsity Minstrels
held down on 6th Street in March
at the Hancock Opera House
held captive on his dormitory's cold third floor
where before it rose so high the water froze
yet flies were fewer than back at home
at the dairy farm on Joshua Creek
where the milk he hated
drew those lifelong enemies
though others swore
his worst was he himself
even if trained & became a star athlete
whose ascetic ways paid off each year
at the State Track meet
from biking to the Alamo

running to Mount Bonnell & back
"a funny sort of a boy"
sat there composing at sunset
poems on the Texas norther
"comes sudden and soon
At the dead of night or the blaze of noon"
or during the small-pox epidemic
of Please anything but my vaccinated arm
"O the day was made for study
But the night for mirth and song"
on the choir trip to Palestine by train
made goo-goo eyes at all the gals
a handsome guy & yet he talked
like "a cripple trying to walk"
his loyalty & zeal surpassed
any gift for carrying a tune
first took up the violin
but "swung such a squeaky bow"
his parents sent him out to practice
way far off by the farm's dry well
near the hole where a ranch hand &
his horse fell in
found them on a sighting of buzzards
wheeling high overhead
a spooky spot to all the kids
to Grace Prather the President's daughter
his poetry too gloomy in tone
too pessimistic
he however never doubted himself
it was just that he would put it all off
as if he knew how anything written
might boomerang
then left for Greenwich Village
as have so many since

till now our eyes are all on him
but a judgment each must bear
the "livelong day"
have frittered our time away
talking the part
Bedichek never forgave
preferred him early starved to death
than failing to give us
immortal verse
"He had the voice of Keats"
but who's to compete
with all it's meant
at games & meets with myriad mouths
countless as stars in the midnight skies
singing his joke dead seriously
"till Gabriel blows his horn"
at Corregidor led by General Moore
a rival bunch of Aggies sang his lines
"as a last shout of defiance"
as imperial troops moved in for the kill
give up his blackface lyrics who ever will
nor "Do not think you can escape them"
their "sleepless eyes" keep tireless vigil
expect us to accept no truce no surrender

Potomac Poem

as the river's ice-floes broke
before his boat
he at the prow in his overcoat

high-collared & reaching to his feet
with his three-cornered hat
cocked o so knowingly

Washington crossed the Delaware
like the plan would work
he would reach the shore

& history would forever cheer
for he knew no winter at Valley Forge
could keep him from his rightful place

while today the hero's fiftyish
a balding no-name
with sideburns peppered gray

whose flight from Florida
was downed by snow
& only he with five others

have floated up
all now hanging onto
the broken slippery tail

while from the chopper's cabin
he alone still looks alert
& so they've thrown

the line to him
& yet each time
he's looped it around

a stranger's waist
one next to him
all but frozen

five trips & now
the crew can hardly wait
have never seen nor known

such selflessness
not even in Vietnam
when they lifted the hopelessly hit

while under attack
from every side
at the front & here at home

returning to pick him up
each prepares
his words of praise

circling & circling as
they shape the heartfelt phrase
till staring in disbelief

all search the icy waters
for the slightest sign   any glimmer
spotting here a tennis racket

smashed but bobbing still
there a drowned child's dolly
a shoe   then two

unmatched in size or color
then circle one last time
craning their necks to discover

even a drifting form
to identify at least the face
grown men in a helicopter

wiping their hot wet cheeks
then flying away from
this cold Potomac poem

Wink

bat an eye
& miss its meaning

like dad's advice
to his younger son

who talked of buying
a *Triumph* or such

"why what in hell for?
what would you do tell me

stranded high & dry
no mechanic there understands

or even wants to work on
fancy foreign makes"

wondered why this
insisting so on going

to look for trouble
"it's all over

but mostly where
you can't get to from here

in those parts there *are* no parts
so when that *MG* fails"

his last words of warning
"don't phone me from Wink"

Vidor

is an upright community among the wilds
hardly noticed from the highway splits it
thick with pines & palmettoes hide motor-
boats banks bars every hell-fire sect

here the civilized & the seedy
are sown together in swampy land
though biblical parables need not apply
sex & religion thriving side by side

holy roller meeting times
divide the rainy weeks
half the days for quoting texts
half for fleshly roller rinks

where electric organs service both
for hymning heaven for limbs' animating
skating couples leaping in rainbow lights
or bowed quaking beneath stained-glass panes

out of sight of traffic's judging eye
the two live on as familiar as Spanish moss
earthy unreal as the region's armadillo who's
armored against fed on a common carnal root

Sour Lake

mad at the world
for nothing can even recall
always at those who misunderstood

stomped out of the house
a college dropout at twenty-three
too old still to be running off

yet set on showing them all
would hike by way
of Montana & snow

perspiring then on the Texas coast
or was it Wyoming was headed for
just anywhere west & north

only made it to here some twenty
miles from that Beaumont home
by midnight back in its roses bed

after all those plans for cutting lawns
doing odd jobs from town to town
where friendly folk would welcome

hear this Canterbury tale *astonied*
had made it so far & all alone
to write then from Missoula or Butte

surprise! arrived in one piece it's forty below!
saw it all on leaving the highway road
entering the brush to camp near water

early enough to take some bearings
to build a summer fire & read Thoreau
Walden packed in with the match supply

lasted perhaps an hour past dark
till mosquitoes all-but carted me off
then started for the nearest resort

hitched a ride with a hick hot-rodder
cruised with him around this town
hardly rubbed up against the Big Thicket

woods where men have wandered lost
but never wanted nor needed return
were not at a loss to see it through

had come to touch
what can't be told
nor would it ever have been believed

that kid no romantic bent on revenge
just out looking to pick up tits
dropped me off at the Laundromat

to wait there safely in its electric light
afraid to go further & hurting to admit
wasn't staying not even one night

in dejection retracing those easier steps
with a heavy backward shadow
from moonlight through the leaves

then spotted a sign of neon life
"Hayseed Beer & Dance"
heard the amplified boom of a Western band

like a heart alone deep in the woods
the silent drift of russet needles
piling up as fears at each hoot or rustle

stood there as the couples drove out & in
asked an older set for a lift to the city
to be let off at sellers of oil well supplies

so relieved to breathe again that refinery air
had had enough of such country fragrance
of a trip to a lake of disillusion

this town could keep its sweet-gum ways
its waking to songsters on dogwood limbs
its manna of pine cones & blooming azaleas

Nome

on Highway 90 heading east of Houston
from here China is merely five more miles
from fang-white cold & Klondike gold

a matter of minutes to mandarins clothed
with flame-breathing dragons on brocaded robes
from blizzards & frostbite & blinding light

a few hundred seconds to plum trees' flowering snow
the shortest route for trekking back across
as if by dogsled kayak or tennis-racket shoes

to fireworks & ink from igloos penguins & caribou
two continents brought miraculously close
by neighboring communities still breed & grow

brahma & rice along their flat & marshy coast
named by those hoping to strike a bonanza here
or who aside from cash crop & cattle would throw

I Ching read tea leaves in cookies their fortunes told
proof of a kind of travel relative or telescoped
at one time bound halfway between on Greyhound

home to write against all odds poems in Beaumont
something right out of Ripley's Believe-It-or-Not
when the scene appeared & rendered a clumsy mess

of an owl driven by rainstorm onto windshield glass
stunned & stuck momently crushed & bleeding
then brushed off & out of sight by the wiper's pass

any thought obscured by lame & fractured lines
as through the bird's impact that web of cracks
& could clearly see it had happened the same

from seeking to link the distant & distinct
& yet with revelation would never escape
& thanks to such mercurial metaphorical trips

this & other Texas towns have suddenly meant

Newgulf

the Sulfur Company's mining town
in an area known as Boling Dome
beside their basic beautiful plant
built to be environmentally sound

in '23 Albert Wolf had scouted the site
without any help from modern geophysics
recommended by him as a promising land
the most he found in the whole Gulf coast

the unborn composer's dad phoned at Jonah
"there is work if you can be here by tomorrow"
a Depression job & his Model A out of gas
all four of its old tires slick & flat

no clothes or shoes he could show up in
then outfitted at the nearest dry-goods store
his car too by the father of a boyhood friend
knew he'd pay it back could count on him

served on the survey crew for laying it out
laid off then rehired & returned to houses framed
pecans growing along every lettered street
crape myrtles in rows & most dwellings the same

bar ditches seen from screened-in porches
kept clean by the Company & freshly painted
the lawns all mowed & neatly trimmed
though here his mother never quite at home

his father ever with his minor industrial role
its history of locating & smelting sinewy iron
lustrous silver   icy platinum   glittering gold
while this a nonmetal a virile versatile atom

its extremes present in various sulfide ores
at once powerfully vitriolic & strangely docile
elemental sulfur itself "the stone that burns"
this one of free enterprise's brightest stories

from erecting & striking the derricks' rigging
for "discovery of bodies heretofore unsuspected"
embedded in salt caprocks of its coastal hills
removed by Herman Frasch's revolutionary process

of water superheated for melting deepest deposits
pumped up to the surface by their air compressor
to compete with the Sicilian mines' lower costs
he rising through pipeline ranks to a supervisor

as a driller's helper was where he began
Claude & he both starting at 80 a month
by '57 that buddy at the top as its president
then elected in '68 as chairman of the board

his dad just as happy among expansion joints
where the gauges & spigots creep back & forth
moved up to miss the fitting & welding of leaks
a craft of not tying down but of letting pipe float

his the joy of Success's thousands at her beck & call
not to be pushed but to follow his leadership's pull
like a geologist with eyes impaired knees from football
out after the unchanging not the confusing & fickle

digging in the earth for its hidden treasure
in contact with its wondrous beauty & power
extracted for a standard of living always higher
any profits depending on a resourceful nature

conserved & reclaimed land stripped & drained
turned a forty-foot dome into a recreational lake
letting cattle graze & slowly the timber revive
renewing pastures until even the buffalo thrived

ran the risk of protracted trials appeals rehearings
a Federal case over lengthy misleading complaints
in court defendants on trading of insiders' shares
their "Perpetual Jeopardy" read by students of law

& from here sent their search around the globe
north through iceberg tips of arctic seas
on a whale boat manned by two Eskimos
to the midnight sun of forbidding reaches

south to Mexico's isthmus of Tehuantepec
unsuspicious Nopalapa between Gulf & Pacific
to the outback Iran Iraq Ethiopia & Egypt
the tantalizing Canadian Shield at Kidd Creek

on the lookout for a clue in that summer swamp
frozen in winter below where dreams can probe
drilling through clay & into rock down 600 feet
in the middle of nowhere gambling against all odds

in a helicopter mounted with electromagnetic detector
checked again on readouts for anomalous zig or zag
by the piles of moose bones ketchup & bottles of gin
to strike a bonanza overlooked by a lonely prospector

through heroic adventures on surveying teams
would measure & map & jockey for claims
then their plane struck a mountain on Baffin Island
the geophysicist one ankle dislocated the other fractured

manages to pull others from out of the wreckage
tending to the pilots both critically hurt
till after three days they're spotted & saved
eighteen years later brought into production

through each ordeal runs the perseverance theme
the strongest point by far their survival of disaster
then faced disappearance of the Marine Sulfur Queen
a crew of 39 vanishing traceless between Cuba & Keys

that world's first tanker for moving in liquid form
bound from Beaumont to Norfolk with 15,000 tons
the mystery from those dark days remains unsolved
though by Christmas their sales hit an all-time high

his mother lowest on finding his appetite gone
not eating could ruin his health & threaten his life
then regained it in Wharton at the children's ward
follow-up trips to the pediatrician her only escape

when she'd order her usual at the corner drugstore
a chicken salad sandwich & a fountain limeade
on the drive going & coming her color restored
spirits lifted retelling him of their very first date

then knew they neared home by the sour stench
of mining water running in their drainage ditch
to the son its smokestacks his welcome sign
had arrived at their manicured railroad line

the golf course & club where he first performed
recital pieces shown off before all this town
past the brick post office & along their street
to spot in the sycamore his private tree house

or to turn to the left & cross over the tracks
could read the disabled report's numbers in red
if none a green light on the bulletin board
by memorial flagpole listing World War dead

from Aguilar to Rodríguez while those not taken
served the nation by excavating vital brimstone
capping & sealing the wells with mud & cement
his father out in the fields a foreman by then

meeting the prediction it would yield 50 million
after over 70 of long tons "still agoin' strong"
yellow blocks piled first by wood then metal forms
to his dad its 50-foot-high vat a work of art

retained its golden liquid till solidified dry
up on a surface stadium-like but twice the size
its reserve inventory winning in the Axis game
& freedom in raising the ante had upped its price

pushed production & the stocks to record heights
his hardened slab a vision of Coronado's cities
funded the Houston Symphony for a concert here
through V-Day dividends put its program on the air

constructed the Boy Scouts hut & a reservoir pier
where the son camped & learned to swim & dive
beneath it carved a horse's head on a creosote beam
one of those summers shared with Company friends

among them Nola & Dean & shy Mary López
in overalls & pigtails ever kept her distance
their cabins separated by a big vacant patch
rode his bike there to visit but was not let in

told simply "it's just not done by either side
we have ours & you have your own lives
meet on the job   at school   or at the restaurant
where we feed you Anglos jalapeños & enchiladas"

shut down & now only cattle egrets fly or stand
white sentinels among the weeds & rusting pipe
since a French conglomerate took over the plant
the workers either transferred out or told to retire

his house & so many others hauled off or leveled
managers' row half vacated though still superior
like the director's mansion with its stunted palms
its bungalow for foreign dignitary or state governor

nothing much of this missed in his mother's mind
happier in Beaumont when they moved from it all
each duplicate street   every predictable shift
Company stores decorated with the same reindeer

wanted for him a better a far brighter future
looking back remembered the drawing he'd made
of a keyboard on paper where his fingers played
the phrases he heard & would scribble however

but knew even then he must have the real thing
must study with the only teacher a few blocks away
in their uncertainty they'd drive him to Houston
he impatient for delivery when the lessons began

dashed to her house across neighboring yards
scales repeated with her idols all looking down
busts of Mozart Schubert Tchaikovsky Chopin
loaned him her priceless records & favorite scores

carried him to the opera & introduced the stage
then quickly her technique not up to his own
outgrown though never those gummed gold stars
the reward given by an old maid her piano in view

of the hospital whose expected was a witness to
an elementary watched over & corrected his script
a penmanship would lead to the measureless bars
to notes & ties for a linking of the close & far

a serial composition could explore & invert
as a foreman-father's lines to float & expand
discover a jagged melody in the electronic scan
rise above as smokestack & a mother had urged

his "Cortege for Orchestra" in memory of her
his burden of paying tribute by a 12-tone row
to one lost & mourned in that mysterious Bermuda
no heavier load ever to leave any Texas port

the perpetual risk taken some plaintiff might sue
file for copyright infringement of his minor sixth
misjudge the timbre of which instrument to choose
the peril of notating & transposing a sexual pitch

& yet through harmony & discord coming to prove
how from deepest swamps & most acrid odors
even the smallest place can hope to produce
love's slow procession in triumphal taste

at Kennedy Center performed his "Museum Pieces"
compared in their way with Mussorgsky's *Pictures*
his operatic setting of a Chekhov's *Three Sisters*
recollection of home abandoned of parting kisses

his saxophone quintet & two elegies for flute
rising & falling to feelings' supply & demand
pumping other hearts with emotions heated & cooled
under her influence who taught a pipe-fitter's gang

guided to the Seven of Cíbola by a Mexican's lot
by way of bitter streams to music's Elysian Fields
through soundings of this jerkwater idyllic spot
to empty rooms filled with the unforgettable

Liberty Hill

brutally handcuffed & driven
from here to the county seat
by a sheriff's deputy
at illegal speeds

booked & fingerprinted
locked up in a reeking cell
on orders of a one-armed
Justice of the Peace

whose courtroom behind its bench
sports a pair of famous photos
of Judge Roy Bean's
"Law West of the Pecos"

this just 40 miles northwest
of the capital city
home to high tech & legislature
the State's largest university

car impounded & bail set
all because I had questioned
his taking of the perjured word
of our daughter's abusive jerk

who had jumped the backyard fence
forced the front door open
insulted & threatened since
she said she wouldn't see him again

happened this spring a year ago
now here to attend a dedication
at their International Sculpture Park
I didn't have to return for

yet came to honor Fowler's art
RAF pilot San Antonio born
pioneer jet fighter in Korea & 'Nam
earned a Bronze Star & a Purple Heart

in retirement started his new career
hammering out his "Libertarian"
with arm-like branches bent above
& below a faceless patch of

head-shaped stone bears the cross
lifts high a David's star & a torch
all dated bicentennial July Fourth
signed it simply Mel his tabby too

yellow abstract with pyramid ears
called it "Liberty Cat" of course
legs head & tail displaced but there
to be found like freedom's Cheshire

dead in Italy at 69
fell from a ladder & drowned
facedown in a puddle just inches deep
though had by then fulfilled his dream

his private vision to bring
the nations to Precinct No. 2
to catch them in the creative act
as from a single piece his garden grew

his ashes scattered here as willed
from a vintage Stearman biplane
among his native oaks & hills
where a figure a year would rise or recline

Jean-Paul Phillipe of France's
"Tirez moi de la"
an actual rope in limestone
a soundless kind of Liberty Bell

Mihama from Japan rolled
twisted the rock as dough
log-sized loaves of bread
baked in time's geologic stove

Tom Piccolo's "Blanca mujer"
her torso a type of cello
with cedar beams bolted where
strings could throb pizzicato

Ann Merck's Western nude
her hair in a Victorian bun
on her stomach with buttocks up
fingers touching to shade the sun

an unsigned limbless creature
with its parts separated into three
on one pink surface carved graffiti
toward whose meaning it seems to crawl

Jim Thomas's "Forgotten Ancestors"
bronze cobwebbed cow skull star-
shaped spur-helmeted conquistador
his eye socket pupil a living spider

others by West German Canadian Pole
but now unveil Melville's masterpiece
when dignitaries pay belated tribute
those never thought he'd ever do it

Land Office reps   a Senator's staffer
Endowments & Commissions lent no aid
officials here today to win swing votes
most like the J.P. named but didn't show

as the ribbon's cut citizens ooh & aah
at the blue-grey veined Italian marble
of Mel Fowler's "Misterio di vita"
posthumous gift for the welcome they gave

to Renata Reck came to sculpt & stayed
to Don Cunningham school administrator
who helped to secure this adjacent tract
for their high school museum out-of-doors

to locals who provided tools of the trade
a place to put up & home-cooked meals
from their unmown lots the raw materials
solid sedimentary & metamorphic support

for the daily constructing & chipping away
all captured & preserved on video
by James Vaughn an ex minor-leaguer
now restores steam engines & diner cars

as even in these smallest of kicker towns
have learned to discover at least two sides
first & lasting impressions
Jekylls & Hydes

Kountze

self-advertised as
"the town with a
sense of humor"

more famous around
these conservative parts
for Arch Fullingim's

liberal notes
hot coals
in his weekly *News*

but mostly a milestone
one more on the highway home
merely a joke on speeding through

to Scout or church camp
a delicious swim
in sandy treacherous

Village Creek
or a hunting trip near
like the one for squirrel

when awaited with the
safety off a shot already knew
would surely miss

no good with a gun
unable even to stomach
the imagined sight of

a bloodied living thing
when dad decided
to smoke him out

to set a small twig fire
at the base of the inverted
v-shaped hole

of a hollow tree
had seen him scamper & take to
till it caught inside

blazed out of control
watched as the flames
leaped limb to limb

suddenly engulfed
that whole
dead trunk

but on driving back
dad saying not to worry
it wouldn't catch the woods

yet thoughts went red & black
filling up with infernal clouds
could see & then could hear

the forest floor ignite
a roar sent up by every acre
& through his decision not to phone

to a Ranger lookout station
could picture charred stumps
of pecan & pine

all this now a kind of historical marker
no granite slab with a metal seal
in the State's panhandle shape

bearing that month day & year
but on the map of routes
dirt or paved

of the roads
to love & trust
a memory

smoldering yet
would just as soon forget
nothing more's

worth naming here
unless it's perhaps
a performance on

their dew-wet football field
when our marching band
took first division

or the date from this country place
whose father ran a filling station
with clean inspected restrooms

its *Mosinee* towels
its liquid soap a yellow-green
& the key like *Pennzoil*

"asked for"
she a Methodist
wouldn't kiss if implored

sitting long hours at a drive-in screen
through wildly impassioned Hollywood scenes
prayed they would rage & spread to her

but that too a fire in a hollow tree
was to burn itself so quickly out
the way all along he said it would

another minor landmark
known only as
good for a laugh

Houston

the air heavy with wet
heavier on a bright muggy day
when mosquitoes floated
out of the bayou mouths
in thick humming breaths
swarming so you would nearly choke
or if not   then gag on chemical clouds
of the fumigator's nightly spray

it was a weather stuck with you
more than men   everything
was close   clothes in summer
sucking the sweat   gray sky kissing
the morning mist   closets of damp & mildew
apartments compact as hives
though honeyless   everything close   except the lives
those   more often asunder

a stadium of voices from every state
urgent accents from East & West
a U. of Michigan graduate
once linebacker on a Rose Bowl team
turned a 9-to-5er in a bruising Bank & Trust
or the man Prudential Insurance moved
with wife & kids   from their Connecticut dream
reshowing the Hartford slides hoping it somehow soothed

come to a complex from the country   the only Texans there
our pup   a few months old   blown apart
by the dogcatcher's high-powered legal weapon

the church bazaar & cakewalk
on an asphalt court of St. Vincent de Paul
when allowance went for naught
the junior-high dance when would never dare
hold her close   all the days it wasn't fun

rules seemed so hard to learn
multiplication tables bored
swimming nude made the cheeks burn
in games only the bullies scored
& then   any lessons were lost on weekends
when nothing made half as much sense
as trading the kid with a Mohawk strip for Batman comic books
or watching on that first TV "Boston Blackie" catching crooks

in adjacent woods all knew how red & black
was a friend of Jack
how red & yellow
could kill a fellow
yet on the streets or in the halls
could never quite distinguish
all   red black or white   seemed corals
cold snakes of injustice

even knowing the names of trees
memorizing dates   i's before or after e's
made nothing right or easier
the girl with rheumatic fever
who could never leave her room
only the half-wit spoke with her
mashing his nose against the screen
once recovered she found him a bother

but enough of this
every ledger has another side
& on it one can list
those have made it a matter of pride
to have spent eight months in this metropolis   though known
more for NASA & the artificial turf of the Astrodome
than for those converted to countless gain
their long nights of loneliness & pain

think of Bracker that longtime friend
who wrote of life with his father here
in a simple four-line poem that pays
true homage to the man & his tender ways
recall how Vassar Miller's sonnets mend
a broken spirit   taking care
the boney wisdom   the metered touch   offset
a body born in the red

hear Stokowski & the symphony orchestra
heaping the city's treasure store
with an Ives or a Villa-Lobos score
& after Barbara Jordan's puissant speech   hurrah!
for the election gave her a seat   more for the vote she cast
to bring men closer than a humid coastal climate
enter them all as accounts receivable   a balancing of hate
a summing in solvent black what once appeared but a bankrupt past

Honey Island

not far from Sour Lake
it never is
for in this State as anywhere

the same farm road
can always lead
from sweet to bitter   bitter to sweet

those early settlers stuck such names
on our Texas towns & cities
though in each the memories & meanings change

since just as one will envision at times
an inviting isle   an Atlantis jewel
in a stagnant pond of a setting

so in the one the other may dwell
a transmuting of land or water
depending most on who was there

& if she went along
to boat or swim
or stole away with another

sneaking off to skinny dip
or paddled out with him
to splendor in the grass

left behind on the green-scummed shore
or given such looks as sent one rowing alone
to some mired mosquito grove

as when the class took its senior trip
to a picnic beside these double pools
where the girls let down their hair

showed more than cheerleaders at pep-rallies
doing splits   forming a pyramid tip
while the jocks all bared their chests

dangling from the high-dive board
by chinning to flex
their bronzed biceps

coveted all they had
their perfect flips & jack-knives
their lovely breast & butterfly strokes

yet dreamed of something more
knew even then could never sport
brains to match their brawn or beauty

only feelings forever feared to show
a hopeless love that surely stood out
as clearly as all their parts

bulging in tight bikini trunks
or shapely in strapless bathing suits
till time has slowly conceived a line

not one intends to impress
the way they won their hottest dates
but one to record & return that day

for this go-round by reading aright
the highway sign to its Thicket knoll
am getting & having it again

as here above the towering pines
have stopped the sun
to let it shine

off emeralds liquefied
off ambered skins aglow
with a tan will still survive

long winters after the last of those
believing their lives spent & over
have lost all sight of this paradise

& by a word-hoard recompense
with its pleasure-pained recall
to bring it back tenfold

Fort Worth

The Stockyards

the place of death
where the bright free age of grazing grass
where the trails & rails led & it came to pass
a hammer's blow snuffed their need for breath

is a half-suspected self
avoided as that avenue at night
known as "cut & shoot"   where winos rent at the famed Right
a hotel roomed ranchers   now but those who are on the shelf

of the many have gone & left
in search of art or peace   those born & raised
in Cowtown too   who pulled up stakes
I alone stand here now   strangely bereft

staring at where the packing-house shell
looms cold & burnt   its panes all cracked
with ladders scaling roofless walls   smokeless stacks
alone to account or make up for a kind of hell

could not be faced   like General Meade
chasing Mexicans to make them take it back   Texas   Hades
others escaped this "culture gulch" by heading East
to write off what gave roots as just bad seed

like those acknowledged little or none
of what went on   knew it more as myth
than any way of life willed or lived with
all the while having steak   eating t-bone

till on this ninety-degree day have come to overlook
two branches of the Trinity River
to watch from bluffs Clear & West forks gather
where the Comanche camped   took

his time   pitching his symboled tent
unperturbed by twisters drifting around
believing nothing would ever let them touch down
not here   a sacred spot   taken over since by the Power Plant

now driving down the viaduct
descend to what was once a ritzy section
given over since to Boys Clubs   Golden Gloves   Mexican
food-to-go   coming next to the Livestock

Exchange   a sand-colored structure
still a stop for cattle buyers   its style
of Arabic arches & red Spanish tile
houses sellers of sheep & hogs   a poster picture

of a champion steer   & out the back
its steps caked with half-digested hay
raked off handmade boots   lead to charolais
short horn   white face   black

angus   an auction arena   an amphitheater
with its ribbed silver-painted fence
a half octagon holding ephemeral prints
of hooves destined to patch the dinnerware

with their mucous-colored glue
the dirt on the stage-like floor trampled powder soft
the performance attended by rows & rows of off-
white straws   hats stained by rain & sweat   not a shoe

on any foot   the show begins when the electric doors
swing to welcome them in   bunches of half-grown cows
frightened as amateur actors   announced to the house
by the auctioneer singing a song of trills & figures

"Gi' me a half gi' me
Got 24 gi' me a quarter
25 need a quarter
29.75 now 30"

two men with long smooth sticks
herding the group   hitting it hard
till bidding done   when exits part
close on rears   give fearful kicks

outside among the pens whips crack
driving them in   long trucks backed up
to loading chutes   cattle cars cou-
pled beside the branding lots   then the pack-

ing house   its name in red & white
though SWIFT has faded   crumbled down to IFT
a mass of wires & rods   twisted
doubled rusted pipe

reaching into rubble   the fire-
ravaged brick as if bombed out
though no atom has fallen here   no Kraut
or Jap has returned the favor to Convair

today General Dynamics   whose B-24s in squadron
sprouted engulfing clouds   here first spread their wings
to fly not with grain but deadly droppings
while up this wooden incline longhorns waited in line

moved slowly to the slaughter   the fire "an accident"
burned for months in consuming the blood & fat
a seeping down would soak the wood   the mat-
ted hides   the conflagration hardly making a dent

in the years of calf eyes crushed to bleed
sadly bright on flaying floors   the nightly flames
razing the ruins   emblazoning brands   oily brains
swollen tongues sputtering until all must heed

the meaning of this chapter   this hidden life
none has ever cared or dared to come upon
not old-fashioned   written by a time gone
by   but that each finds his fingers fit the knife

formed this sloping passage spared by tribal spirits
rising still to a gutted   a caved-in corporation
remembrance of even a risen sun's
decline   kinetics the seeming-innocent drive inherits

in reconciling past & present a ramp
for rendering down to what we've been & are
for ascending higher than a bigger spread   a grand Lone Star
setting instead on less an ancient sanctioned stamp

Denton

like every other place
is Janus-faced
take its dreamed-of campus Kenton blessed
near where an only brother bled to death
on his final trip from picking up a remaining group
of Green Beret reservists the last to parachute

delivered them safely then flipped his truck
on a narrow curve   his stomach crushed
between the driver's seat & the steering wheel
for years have grieved with that lonely feel
of his young life slipping away
three months after graduation two weeks before his wedding day

talked Aunt Sis into taking a pilgrimage to its hallowed sounds
in summer heat to its celebrated tree-cooled grounds
home to festivals a division of Columbia Records pressed
like this treasured album has stood the test
though scratchy & so filled with cuts by imitative combos
a true aficionado would not confess he even knows

much less still listens to its Euel Box Quintet
on "Toddlin'" or "Woodchoppers Ball"   the only regret
never to have caught them in live performance
here in this town for that final chance
for afterwards the valve-trombonist-leader would graduate
see his sax & trumpet his bass & drums all go their separate

ways to public schools where jazz is seldom heard
to some a discouraging word
few on the road with Herman or Stan a record date with those

203

fewer as first chair with East or West Coast studios
can only hope wherever they went
each made music on his chosen instrument

their talents might have been or maybe not
the equal of a fellow alum's like Giuffre whom none forgot
from here Jimmy had gone to join those idols' bands
to star with Shorty Rogers on Atlantic's *Martians*
Come Back   his name listed in liner notes
with the likes of a Mingus   his tune set off in quotes

his famous "Four Brothers"   am left now with not even one
stranded on the outskirts forever of marriage & the job he'd won
never to share with his bride
a game of golf at the Country Club laid out beside
the Trinity River   nor to practice on his trap set for another gig
as drummer to roughnecks off an oilfield rig

An Occasional Ode

teachers of a second tongue
have come to Spain for '92
to this land brought change
to the map & language too

whole lives as well
those of others
for better or worse
only they can tell

but these for certain
would count the wealth
of a blend of words
mosarabic to Salamancan

to catch them have listened close
to the Madrilenian lips
of professors Olga & Piedad
they on tours the patient guides

steering where & how to partake
of monastery aqueduct & synagogue
to drink in stained-glass light
arts of ribbed dome & flying buttress

delivering their learned lectures
on Goya   El Greco   Velásquez
Picasso   Sorolla   El Escorial
their enthusiasm ever contagious

their deep delightful insights

filling these foreign eyes & ears
with the colors shapes & lines
of a beauty & truth Hispanic style

by night have turned Columbuses under sail
on three dorm-ships: Empresa Pública Mara Isabel
theirs a discovery route now in reverse
travels them back to old world treasures

new ones of custom & phrase
a vocabulary untasted before
in uttering each delicious place
in stuttering it out to savor

to relive the ancient look & feel
of cathedrals castles & cities of fame
Segovia Toledo Cuenca Seville
relished in repeating each name

but how to return the favor
can only hope to half-pronounce
the lilt of *vale vale* from every side
soon for students uneager to learn

those at home will be exposed
to Andalucía through print & slide
cards & posters from El Prado & Casón
zarzuelas heard & the Sevillana tried

their thanks extended to all of these
Guillermo Irina Begoña Adela
Teresa Juan Leticia Luis
Carmen Blanca Paloma Varela

& despite it all to conquistadors
braved   enslaved   & saved
traded   degraded   & remade
till in the end they at last created

a Rubén Darío   Vallejo   & Borges
a Mistral   Neruda   Lihn   & Paz
a Carpentier   & García Márquez
a Parra   Sábato   Puig   & Cortázar

theirs a linguistics richer than gold
the highest grade of an American ore
valued with Cervantes   Unamuno   & Lorca's
for any & every "materials" course

participants in the Quinto Centenario
they'll long gaze backwards & forwards
recall the magic date he sighted land
brought over a subject to understand

if never fully to master
yet to know with love & respect
to impart with passion & pleasure
& in gratitude to Ortega y Gasset

A Bullfight on Color TV

have never been to one
nor would ever want to be
in this or any other arena

but stand here now transfixed
as natives pass along this street
have known it all before

are undisturbed it seems
makes one wonder the more
as they pause & stare

to compare the prices
of this store's imported sets
bearing signs declare a bargain

"reduced" as he will be
to his bloody knees
but only now emerges

with a chartreuse ribbon
fluttering from
his hump beginning to

bleed
as the picadors
tease & run for cover

safe behind
their protective wall
while he

slides in the circle of sand
bangs against the barrier
& stuck now with

another ribboned stick
looking more man than beast
wearing his heart

upon his sleeve
as the toreador takes
his short effeminate steps

decked in sequins
& gold brocade
his thighs in tights a vivid pink

his white shirt
like a ruffled blouse
his shoes like those of ballerinas

with on his lips
a lighter shade of pink
as he holds his bright red cape

to hide the blade
all this somehow meant
to represent

one tormented
by the woman
of his fondest

dreams
but it couldn't be
it must say

something else
appears but the cruelest
bit of flirting

for a crowd approves
when the victim sinks
to receive the

final sword
turn & leave
shamed by having watched

& by the torment of
those have come
expecting love

María's Ark

did it come from Goodwill
or another garage sale in the
subdivision of Anderson Mill

on Public TV the panel Bill
Moyers gathered for *Genesis*
argued whether it meant

a cruel God could even kill
His own creation not of course
Noah & his motley crew

the one family on the block
who followed His rules
as when He said to build it

& Noah did
stocking it up
though the neighbors jeered

to him his God so good
that any not doing His will
was in Middle English *wood*

but even in the surviving
Mystery play
his wife would not leap on

unless her gossips everyone
could all come too

when at last Shem their son

had to drag her aboard
with camels polecats & swine
for the forty days of manure

here the animals are flat
cut out surely on an assembly line
painted dark gray or brown

facing in profile all in pairs
elephants giraffes lions & sheep
& how did the latter get on

how ever did the former fit
all now seeming to move
toward these miniature steps

at rest on the fireplace mantel
up against the hull of this ship
its roofed house set in the middle

to be loaded with symbols
from that biblical tale
its dove of love

its olive of peace
its rainbow sign of
an end to revenge

but just as much
the simple design
of two of each

male & female
climbing on together
knowing her this must have been

what she had in mind
when she spotted
& had to have

her bargain buy

María's Birds

it isn't that the doves jays cardinals or
mockingbirds belong to her
but the feeders & the green plastic bath
she's placed outside this patio window
bring them here whenever they please
to peck at her store-bought sunflower seeds

to dip their beaks or splash their wings
no walls of wire to keep them in
coming & going by their own routine
as always at suppertime they seem to arrive
first one pink-footed dove then six or seven
flapping & maneuvering under the arbor's vines

its grape leaves shading their seeds & water
as each alights atop her larger redwood roof
then hops down onto its platform holds
a box made out of cedar
heaped full with black or empty hulls
the latter if she hasn't replenished

their daily supply
their breasts too big to land or fit upon
the tiny wooden porches
of the smaller closed-in type
with its see-through panes on two
of four rectangular sides

only the chickadees or titmice reaching
to the seeds drop through
an opening beneath the glass

says she'll buy a book to identify
those whose names remain unknown
though recognizes them by their crests

or their slightly reddish bands
as she watches at evening with such delight
while eating her vegan meal
agreeing with Lindbergh who late in life
declared if he had to choose between
the planes he flew

his famous Spirit of St. Louis
& the many models he'd flown in since
would rather have her feathered friends
though how would she visit her people in Chile
of course the neighbors' cats prefer them too
over bags or cans of kitty food

tries shooing them away when they lie in wait
but those will come as free as birds
leap the fence & over potted plants before they fly
leaving in the shrubbery just a span of wings
more often of the taunting mocker
who dares to dive or strut too close

the one each morning who always sang
from the mildew-resistant white crape myrtle
his varied pitches his seemingly endless tones
those caught on coming to bathe or feed
bother her so much more
feels deeply her love has done them in

though every regret remains outweighed
by a need to see their sudden unfathomable flight

this & their colors & their nervous twitches
sketched with kernels & the garden hose
by this artist of the airways whose special guests
put on in her own backyard their death-defying show

María's Hands

her own are nothing like the ones
in El Greco's ecclesiastical portrait
of a Cardinal in red cap cape & lace
rendered with thin elongated fingers
be-ringed & extended on elegant folds
hers although short not stubby at all
of a feminine form yet softly strong
her delicate nails with quarter moons
uncovered with polish or silver glitter
as she peels beets carrots or onions
washes lettuce pot pan or toilet bowl
through whatever they handle or lift
pencils & pens copybooks & spirits
never rise nor set but shine the same
one slightly bent from having it caught
in a bicycle chain left a permanent mark
on her right second digit's larger joint
whose pinky bears a sympathetic bend
is tender at times from her fibromyalgia
on the other hand wears her wedding band
an unadorned gold from a Chilean store
her best friend no sparkling diamond
at another shop on the Square of Arms
had the accepted name engraved inside
only once removed it as her protest sign
on finding its mate taken off from a pain
caused by a golf club swung with it on
never took in school any typing lesson
yet her indices do as much as any two can
on any keyboard always accurate & quick
with gloves on has dug in the hardest dirt

walking or sitting deep comfort has come
from holding them bare if sore just to feel
them laid on mine will ever minister & heal

María's Metempsychosis

not to hear the rude remarks she so resents
says next time around will marry an orphan
be spared those in-laws must always hint
how awfully wrong she has raised her kids

even better will return in an animal's skin
of dog or cat eats & sleeps for half the day
barks or scratches at the door to be let in
to shrieks of delight petted watered & fed

in dishes will never wash dry nor ever fill
yet most gives pause when simply declares
will come back male be done once & for all
with lumps in the breast a fibrous uterus

& what will that leave but a choice between
gay or female & how is that going to feel
whatever shape shade or gender she takes
paired with her again will be nirvana still

María's Radio

keeps her company & up to date
entertains her as she cooks & bakes
marathons in advance of weekly meals
each delicious dish will nourish & fill
the curried chicken over a bed of rice
Texmati or jasmine with an onion slice
first skinned deboned & boiled to a froth
to make the base for a tasty natural broth
for homemade soups of her vegetable mix
or of spinach alone so healthful & iron rich

her favorites the local Scot announcer-singer
Ed Miller on "Folkways" & Garrison Keillor's
"Prairie Home Companion" Terry Gross too
with knowns & unknowns she will interview
on "Fresh Air" & "Car Talk's" philosophical
grease-monkey brothers who at every call
yuk it up as they dispense advice on muf-
fler ignition switch hydraulic lift along with love
together on NPR with "All Things Considered"
whiling away the only hours ever hear her dread
those spent starching & pressing blouses & shirts
will catch but bits & pieces yet it always irks
on just passing through to the "reading room"
where only jazz & classics would ever presume
resent not so much that pathetic Scotch-Gaelic whine
but rather Paul Ray's program of "Twine Time"

worse than Keillor's satirical lives of cowboys
horse-backed megabites in woe-begone voice
for it's Ray returns to mind her teenage years

Sixteen Candles The Great Pretender Tears
on My Pillow Twilight Time or *Party Doll*
when on slow numbers she will still recall
how Jaime invited her great dancer bigger tease
with parents permitting no Gentile steadies
see her rocking in his arms around the clock
to *Itsy Bitsy Teenie Weenie Yellow Polka Dot*
Bikini It's My Party Little Darling Only You
till the green-eyed beast again breaks through
almost prefer at seventeen she *had* become
as she vowed she would a noiseless nun
no longer to judge a date by socks he wore
how well he could clutch or in soccer score

though in those days not there only later met
she already twenty-two & knew she was get-
ting a gringo stepped on toes & couldn't sing
couldn't stand his own forebears' Highland fling
a Texan given to the darkest of Irish moods
not half so smart nor clever as all those Jews
she's ever admired & yet will share the shows
that I may learn through her of trumpet solos
by Marvin "Hannibal" Peterson of Smithville
then ride in our son's Fairmont cherry mobile
to San Antone & hear with him that live quartet
perform with their orchestra *African Portraits*
will insist that I hurry out of the gloom & listen
to Billy Taylor analyze on "Morning Edition"
Strayhorn's *Lush Life* with its amazing changes
such progressive harmonies as she too arranges

María's Sewing Machine

is heavy enough
to have carried it
as far as she

would have given
most men a hernia
for certain me

she making it through
Santiago & Lima
on then to Miami

where at customs
on purpose
she chose

a Spanish-speaking
official with his
neck encased in foam

couldn't bend
to inspect her bulg-
ing luggage con-

tained her treadle
her cast-iron heritage
with its top of warped

& cracking wood
not to be sold to
the highest bidder

wouldn't trade it in
for the latest *Singer*
with fancy attachments

she tied to this
by all her blood
her youth & childhood

am to her
as bobbin
to thread

together
come what may
will sing her

through every age
who can alter
any cloth

hem or reupholster
slipcover
couch or chair

& with her
sense
of humor

leaves me
in stitches
of love

María's Tambourine Man

having to hear his harmonica & guitar & smart-
assed voice day after day's not the worst part
nor watching in the bedroom as the little space
shrinks while his shrine fills with bootleg base-
ment tapes books like *Song & Dance Man III*
his Brit tour on video re-releases any new CD

nor is it having to hear her *Rolling Stone* read
on a fan dumpster-diving to recover cigarette
butts for DNA to clone Dylan once he's done
digging in trash for any song draft he rejected
to listen to more sightings from bobolinkdotnet
or countless biblical allusions in "Highway 61"

rather it's having about the house a superstar
whose lyrics she's gotten by heart *that* is far
worse or in conversation working in a phrase
of his when labored lines dedicated to praise
her every feature still remain unmemorized
unattended unlike his concerts so apprized

by millions swoon yelling his precious name
throwing any item hoping he'll only touch it
toss it back miraculously with his autograph
yet even with all his followers & all his fame
he hasn't heard or put together how much it
means her hummed "It Takes a Lot to Laugh"

how her "Slow Train Coming" can stop a cry
& her "Man Gave Names to All the Animals"
whistled can change the times or turn a blues

& "Desolation Row" from lowdown to high
tried tuning him out swearing flat denials
was worth the trouble could accept Jews

in jazz & classical even in Tin Pan Alley
but not one aping folksy Woodie Guthrie
every prejudice fallen on sweet deaf ears
she the best defender for a hopeless case
will win it by a look on her zealous face
by a music she's made of all these years

Isabella's Pebbles

barefooted she repeats the word
over & over pebble pebble pebble
wonder why perhaps because

at sixteen months
she thinks by this
to count so many

not even both hands
can hold them all
these shoveled & spread

for this walk between
her *abuelita*'s salvia beds
watered & now inviting

fingers & thumbs to dig
in soft dark mud
can stick to her skin

unlike her fascinating gravel
hard dry & solid
& will never wilt

as leaves she picks
or the yellow corollas
she pulls & sniffs

saying the word again
with each fist full
then lets them fall

drop one by one
to join their fellows
on this garden path

gathers up some more
then repeats as if
Demosthenes upon the shore

teaching himself to speak
against the Mediterranean roar
though she's been sternly warned

never to put them
in her tiny mouth
then gabbles the word again

one of her first
so far a favorite
& maybe it's since

there seems no end
to shapes & colors
beneath her feet

so smooth to the touch
its sound the same
as all it names

though soon enough she'll know
if not the geology
has made them so

the way they're called
in her mommy's Spanish
her daddy's Portuguese

besides this Texas English
she insists on saying over & over
who has heard all three

from lips of parents
were brought together
mysteriously from out of the many

goddess-like she now returns
to her special pair
an oblong white

& a tannish pink
her sharp eye spotting
selecting & placing each

in this larger palm
to keep them safe
for a secret need

Of "Guernica" for Solo Viola by William Penn

a contemporary composers show on PBS
the announcer asks the obvious
Descended from that Quaker man?
Answer: No relation
took his doctorate at 31
from Western Michigan

in the same athletic conference as N.I.U.
played them football in drifting snow
cold schooling in Kalamazoo
so numbing with temperatures sub-zero
Spain is in the south & in the sun
Answer: No relation

the soloist a sophomore
a mere three weeks he had the score
his performance flawless
Penn explains: women weep bombs fall the whole mess
ears perk up at every note
wonder most at how warm he wrote

Civil War for viola   the instrument right
a mellow wooden box subtler as it soars
melody out of massacre
with its runs reach for the light
marvel at the mind the musician admire
a queer liaison William Penn & war

how could an American know the score
how connect the long pass with Picasso
how did Guernica take it stopping for college at 10 below

Kalamazoo
& viola too
a wet-behind-the-ears sophomore

has cartoon America learned to feel
sounds unreal
yet hear it even as wind the flakes do blow
what's more on radio
with Larry Dutton violist & special thanks to Wm.'s pen
a music-making has made Kalamazoo & Pablo kin

The Pilgrimage

began at 7:20 a.m. Austin-Bergstrom
December 20th two thousand & one
on American flight 24   0   9
two planes that airline lost
on September 11th to terrorism
brought the Twin Towers down
though in a way it began in '59
when *Pulse* printed that essay on him
as a pioneer & later wrote in '61
"Order of Worship" that early poem

at first María felt too afraid to fly
then feared it would be too far to drive
weather in the east so unpredictable
the car without any chains or snow tires
tickets bought in August nonrefundable
in the end she decided to risk it
even willing at last to leave alone
on December 10th for Avon
to help Elisa with Christmas
the granddaughters turning 3 & 6

ten days later I would join them all
Newton & Darío & Jennifer too
landing in Hartford where at Nook Farm
Twain had written *The Gilded Age*
Stevens walked to work up Asylum Hill
but didn't manage to see either one
with only a week & most of the days
filled with observing the girls at play
fighting over who would carry the cat
yet determined at least to take that trip

Jenny would baby-sit the younger sister
Newton said he'd seen the town before
on traveling I-84 to meet with clients
in his job with National Instruments
the rest would pack in Elisa's van
head down the roadway lined with pine
here & there a birch with whitest bark
past the campus of a community college
named Tunxis after the Indian tribe
could imagine its wild idyllic life

among the woods on either side
outcroppings of a reddish rock
Darío saying he'd heard or read
for such a rich state Connecticut had
the highest percentage of working poor
remembered then the tourist brochure
in celebration of its "Quiet Spaces"
yet knew in '39 the composer disappointed
on revisiting his once "lively" birthplace
found it so changed had never returned

but still came hoping to view his home
the Housatonic Valley inspired his "grand
and glorious noise" passing just then over
its river known from his aural depiction
his vivid *Three Places in New England*
brought back a synesthetic vision of bands
marching & playing their differing strains
crossing & creating a polytonal dissonance
captured in notes he had set down at night
as with Stevens after a day of insurance

stopped for directions at a service station
a Pakistani saying keep on White to Main

turned left & parked at the Savings Bank
where bells of the Congregational Church
once range out of tune such a delight to him
& to his father had on piano copied them
both hearing the gospel across Chapel Place
at now Danbury National Bank at 210 Main
born on the spot in '74 & living there till '79
when the family moved to the intersection of

Stevens Street with Harmony & there till '89
then back to Chapel Place's renovated barn
listening for five years before he left for Yale
just a paved parking lot the only thing there
the homestead pump organ & steeple gone
the house moved to South & Mountainville
got back in the van & continued up Main
after missing the sign with his faded name
turned around & found his desolate home
the 1790 Dutch colonial in need of paint

pulled into the drive behind a panel truck
from which a workman emerging proved
unfriendly when asked for a peek inside
said "There's nothing here" yet advertised
its carved music stand a gift of his wife
his death mask & on-loan Pulitzer Prize
took one photograph in the dimming light
then Darío insisted we go locate the grave
so drove at dusk in search of a Section M
in the cemetery where overlooking a pond

Charles Ives lies beside his Harmony
but couldn't find it gave up & went on
to Dunkin' Donuts to use its restroom
where a teenager with a ring in her nose

brought back how prophetic that street
with her very same name though to most
instead of Harmony he'd married discord
at best merely repeated snatches of hymns
quoted again "The Battle Cry of Freedom"
or "Come Thou Font of Every Blessing"

with Elisa at the wheel I peered into the dark
at Waterbury's lights on passing back through
wondering if by any chance the Pakistani knew
his *Concord Sonata* if that teenager were to hear
his *Symphony #3* or *Robert Browning Overture*
would she convert from body piercing to faith in
his transcendental notes for not having even seen
stand or gravestone reverence had been renewed
& in Texas would soon put on *The Unanswered
Question* & "In the Barn" from *Violin Sonata #2*

Fessing Up to David Yates

Ure aeghwylc sceal   ende gebidan
worolde lifes. . . . – *Beowulf* (ll. 1386-87)

miss you most because   & must admit it
your magazine meant   a place to publish
a form of self-love   another by-line craved
though more so now   than ever before
since at your going   your tabloid folded
had opened to   the priceless poems
at times a photo   when you chose to run it
of your own face's inner glow   a pose in that final number
no mirror will ever return   your white hair long & premature
though no sign there   of any ruptured disc
of pain or pills had pushed you   instead of proofing
others through the press   to pipe exhaust fumes in

would await the postman   for each new issue
to find unknowns   their metaphors o so fresh
could make the day   or save it from
a feeling any food   fast or grown organic
was such a waste   could never really feed
as the words you penned   of a recipe for making bread
of a cow skull's smile   from its yellow teeth you brushed
of Dickey's independence   his announcement to all
then flopped facedown   smack-dab in the middle of the street
his friends getting him into bed   to let him sleep it off
of the elderly ignored   Stafford's story of snickersnee
of West Texas wind   you compared to sex
need them more & more   yet must confess
poets as good have come along   even then were here

but your editing & essays   there's none to replace
that where to write to   your address on Madeleine
its road overlooked   your logo's cedar & rock
for mailing of manuscripts   those hopeless lines
held close in hands to drink them in   when all the others
would shoot them back   only you to send acceptance

ask shamefully then   that you forgive & forget
though cannot do   the same for you
unable to live   with the way you left
after you'd written in public   to stay in touch
even failed to phone   or listen to Stokesbury said
to take a later flight   just pulled out sudden-like
the red flag not yet up   ticks still on the meter
all would've dropped & run   as any Minute Man
assembled as the Amish   at the clanging bell
now each grieving image-loss   on a newsprint page
of those inked-up verses   their life-blood vital
an obsession yes   the one you set aside
yet a rejection slip   can still not read

Teachers at South Park High

those still alive invited to 2002's 45th reunion
but of the five attended didn't take from any
one wouldn't make it with his aluminum brain

most unheard of since graduation of the many
had departed the favorite having gone the year
before & yet every face has come back funny

or earnest from nine long months of appear-
ing at the heads of rows for the calling of roll
going over a grammar point remains unclear

all the lessons can't recall to save one's soul
though each body retains what he or she wore
all the quirks & tics days they'd lose control

when interrupted & talked out of turn or more
often the questions unheard too witty to learn
certainly from losers considered a deadly bore

now remembered then merely intent on spurn-
ing not alone subjects but their old fogey looks
fashion & make-up meaning most to undiscern-

ing hotshot know-it-alls wouldn't crack a book
education so uncool & wasted would later say
on the foolish young unprepared to read *Huck*

Finn would now start over ready finally to pay
attention memorize driest dates work equations
yet can only regret it all on a laser-printed page

2 Rachel Dean

with her classes she would always share
those memories from her Mexico days
when a dashing caballero serenaded her

sang from a street below & then sent up
fresh roses filled a bathtub in her pensión
would speak too of & even demonstrated

the Mexican hat dance their *jarabe tapatío*
whirling about as her handkerchief twirled
to sounds of the guitar she once had heard

with the old maid's back turned poked fun
at her romantic delusions so unconcerned
with conjugating of any subjunctive verb

pronouncing volcanoes' nostalgic names
making the male or female ending agree
placing of an accent on the proper vowel

what wouldn't give to chat with her now
in that tongue have come to love so well
even blending a gringo's with latin blood

admit she was right to remember that tub
to wear their colorful embroidered skirts
to have club members peddle Xmas cards

for a trip in winter across that rio border
didn't go after all but had sold the most
demanded the profits from generous her

3 E.O. Lively

indignant to find any man would teach
a class studs said was meant for sissies
those would elect not to take his course

later to pay for a messy expensive typist
but jeered back then at his potbelly waist
snickered whenever once again he'd stick

his hand in the candy machine while those
who signed up & tried to erase the mistake
were always caught soon as he would hold

yellow sheets to the light & spot the place
where paper was thinner & if any thought
to cut off misspellings he would dig them

out of the trash & for such offenses made
to stand in the hall their heads in lockers
one foot in a wastebasket till hour's end

with gum on noses for those who chewed
carriage returns timed to a record played
his "Blueberry Hill" or "One Mint Julep"

he himself cradled & bowed an air violin
tonguing his finger & touching his cheek
to imitate teardrops of girls would plead

that he not count off for just one erasure
reduced their speed the racier sort invited

to wear baby dolls at his slumber parties

4 Eppie Quicksall

with names a quixotic mix of the epic & hick
high-collared blouse & protruding front teeth
a flowery skirt it all made her a laughing stock

as she'd trace Americans by periods & dates
from puritan pre-destiny through colonial rule
to the killing fields of the war between states

in the summer she would tour the battle sites
Vicksburg's row on row of moss-hung graves
Gettysburg's gentle hills where Confederates

met their match & Abe's two-minute address
said it forever whereas for hours would raise
her voice when none would listen her classes

paying for subscriptions to *Senior Scholastic*
at 10 cents each its quizzes on current events
Nasser seizes Suez Canal the polls favor Ike

vocabulary words drawn from a Soviet block
sports maps import-graphs tips on etiquette
letters to the editor the rating of a latest flick

reports on rock & roll rhythms causing riots
on a Nobel Prize discovery in a human heart
thought hers too ancient for having the hots

for any but those had eons ago already died
amazed to learn how late in life she married
gave up History to become a blushing bride

had it been an elective unrequired to graduate
whoever would have chosen to take from him
his course with a title warned will regurgitate

from dissected frogs & learning dots on wings
of monarchs as blue jays do a biologic's bitter
but even with a microscope's lens for looking

at amoeba couldn't see a thing only wonder-
ing if with his thickest of glasses he ever saw
the miniscule labels for ear's stirrup hammer

or anvil whose cochleal tubing made to draw
yet apathetic where the canals led had rather
hear & play beguine notes of an Artie Shaw

than to know near or farsighted didn't matter
not at all just wanting eye-hand coordination
could read & perform parts as a second chair

can't remember if he taught equine evolution
from three-toed into a single hoof or thought
Darwin mistaken & held to a special creation

by then science knew the DNA if he brought
it up tested spelling enzyme or chromosome
don't recall just phoning neighbors' daugh-

ters for Saturday dates later the senior prom
struggled to adapt make the natural selection
be different with all cells of the same system

6 Leola Landers

like the Wife of Bath in Chaucer's Prologue
whose opening verse paragraph memorized
with its rhyming couplets & London brogue

she too was gat-toothed told how it signified
lecherousness but couldn't conceive it in her
so tall overbearing & didn't even try to hide

a wart visible in a V of suede or calf-leather
pump watched it as she read another sonnet
or a Grecian ode fascinated more than either

as she droned on followed her foot saw it fit
right in the V better than poet can fill a form
the best assignment she ever gave was Write

an essay on any theme & so this schoolmarm
got a dissertation on snuff after Lamb's roast
pig which unlike a man is good in every part

but of course she found sniffing tobacco most
unacceptable as a subject for an English class
& deducted points for clearly having grossed

her out then book reports due if hoped to pass
when asked if half a 1200-page novel'd count
since time was running out replied in her sas-

sy way You'll flunk out of college & amount
to nothing & the shoe did fit but luckily saved
by a major in Lit of many a blessing the fount

In Memoriam: Winfred S. Emmons

a practicing Southern Baptist
with an unlikely sense of humor
who loved Geoff Chaucer best
the raunchier he was the better

as when the angry Host bristles
tells the Pardoner he just wishes
he had aholt of his little testicles
says to this peddler of religious

relics charges for kissing a stain
on dirtied drawers he would fain
cut the scrawny pair & enshrine
them both in the turd of a swine

frost on a mule's the metaphor
Win used for that first mustache
tried to grow as his sophomore
next day shaved it by breakfast

selected for his course in British
Lit a Blake-to-present anthology
didn't include "To Nobodaddy"
but recited it himself with relish

not too long after he had gone
took down his monograph on
Katherine Anne Porter whose
Texas stories he could choose

over "The Chimney Sweeper"
said the 'weep made it weaker
how disagree with this mentor
who inspired in the '60 winter

to imitate a Yeats he assigned
next year in an annual picture
is shown already with hairline
receding into a perennial burr

one of his Ethel's photographs
he in the front at that decadent
lounging Roman-style banquet
of her high school Latin class

in another at the football game
she's leading a yell in her dead
language Robert Nossen recom-
mended Study with her he said

& I did but just a private lesson
or two then took off for Austin
where had it first with Jim Hitt
& later on with Christian Smith

had not learned much from her
too short a time only remember
how she'd apply above the line
of her upper lip a ruby *Revlon*

as for Win can see the twinkle
& hear his high-pitched laugh
in translating the Miller's Tale
when a coed got the paragraph

of Nicolas breaking wind how
Absolon pokes the hot plough-
share & burns off his ers's skin
Nick's love for Alison yqueynt

a jolly prof who knew his stuff
from *Hamlet* to the Dick Tracy
comic strip mostly B.O. Plenty
James Joyce & Virginia Woolf

in his Advanced Grammar gave
a poem to diagram can imagine
the prepositions in Sonnet 129
phrasals laid to make one rave

a couplet on his mid-term exam
so tricky a claque of classmates
up nights before trying to cram
was one of his special delights

to some such woe proved bliss
others called it a perfect waste
all they wished was just to pass
finding him in the way of haste

said wouldn't need it for a thing
not planning to teach where else
put it to a single use only Hell's
for passives in living & writing

though can't believe he's there
sure he was not condemned for
being a wit or inclined to savor
scatological rhymes his despair

not a Red Crosse knight's saved
by his Una's cutting words from
giving in to Duessa's rusty blade
in *The Fairie Queene* Book One

Win's rather from slaving on half
the pay of the CEO held no Ph.D.
rendering eke & wight year after
year grading papers so unworthy

losing patience with her atrocious
Thesis then plied a mean red pen
marking it up almost murderous
found him at home with swollen

legs sitting there so sore & bitter
more from being asked to resign
eyes missing their wonted shine
with final days no joking matter

his face minus its devilish grin
had opened & shown so lustily
to interpret a Robert Browning
his Brother he-he snaps the lily

Ethel silent in her nearby chair
those classrooms three blocks
away their blackboards where
both had shared their classics

his "Michael" her Virgil was
this to what it all came down
a form of puritanical justice
for having slighted a religion

by teaching an unholy empire
a gat-toothed lecherous Wife
of Bath then why even aspire
as Nannie says to any afterlife

though that too's just a fiction
of Porter's he had closely read
a black woman's contradiction
of all the church has ever said

whether a parting hour reveal
the comedy's errors are those
told in some *Canterbury Tale*
or come of believing he arose

what good would it do to say
this merely means to witness
the explications abide & bless
pay homage to his jocular way

O-Yo-De-Lay-Hee-Hoing

on his two-year-old a satin-black
with forehead mark a whitish dot
a bridle Sears & Roebuck bought
he'd drive dogies to a dipping vat

aspiring to cords for alpine vocal
harmonizing vowels as cowhand
not with any falsetto of perpetual
boyhood no castrato's half a man

but a joy in yodeling of every age
from the pygmy African Austrian
Swiss Rumanian & Scandinavian
to campfires out in cactus & sage

hankered to warble as all the men
pictured singing on a silver screen
most often then a Gene Autry sort
no Pickens ever in a Republic part

closest thing to an improvised ride
mockingbird's 50 calls so accused
of copying squeaky gates any type
of peep its repertoire badly abused

while in Witter's Grenstone poems
he's declared the pilfering of tones
creates a medley out of a multitude
a single song hatched from a brood

while a chachalaca'll stick to "stac-
cato cadence" a mocker will "chirp
whistle stutter & yodel" as buzzard
wheels with just a silent dip & tack

could recognize a mellifluous dove
woodpecker's tap on a hollow trunk
learned each sound as any Audubon
a Longoria with his brushlands love

hearing her choir do "Precious Lord"
that joyful noise at Sunday's service
always choked up Alfreda Inglehart
K too attended the sanctified church

its swaying congregation patting feet
clapping hands in humid August heat
to hymns soldiering onward in Christ
in the *Elmer Gantry* film its cornetist

leads choir helped André Previn win
an Oscar for his lofty score & on *My
Fair Lady* a hard swinger as he'd fly
across his keys to drum-bass Friends

but traded jazz piano for a London
gig of Rachmaninoff works as con-
ductor of Sergei's *Symphony No. 3
Isle of the Dead* a *"Crag" Fantasy*

that '60 movie based on just a sole
Sinclair Lewis episode a repetitive
plot about its likable but seductive
preacher Lancaster in Elmer's role

but largely changed from the novel
like Sister Sharon played by pretty
Jean Simmons quitting the revival
or she says she will & even marry

yet persisting tent catches fire with
her inside Burt forgiving panicked
knocked her down rushing to save
sinful lives over which she prayed

when K's Pop would speak of God
he couldn't accept poor being good
if wealthy gained from fruits of evil
a heavenly hope made life tolerable

here on earth but said unworthwhile
lost religion found it all too political
compared it to booking agent who's
out for self not for sake of the muse

but's getting ahead has first to touch
his Sis Eva Lois' keyboard on which
she learned pieces attending Lincoln
High in Palestine played for bottling

companies for a Dr. Pepper of Waco
for Coca-Cola its weekly hour show
to promote its drink with a selection
of sight-read tunes Handy Ellington

she to prophesy K's always jumpin'
up & down to her music must mean
would grow up a Louis or a Gabriel
bright biblical high-toned archangel

K's "Mack the Knife" of '59 his own
rocking take on song of Weill-Brecht
the piece Papa Dip did with his direct
& unembellished New Orleanian tone

but before bop coming sharecrop bail-
ing of hay & alfalfa pulling boles scal-
ing with weights sacks two times long
as K & the boiling of cane & sorghum

herding a hundred head to local corral
begging handout for that peg-leg hobo
bound for Frisco spied oil lamp's glow
tested first by his Mom forever cordial

from a white bum's yarns K's yearning
to ride the rods to the Mexicans' border
envisioned perhaps Henrik Ibsen's *Peer
Gynt* from "Hall of the Mountain King"

if to Grieg's incidental *Suite* introduced
in school his ears to ski dizzying slopes
of Norway's Gjendin ridge the ice floes
reindeer cracked & Peer in hot pursuit

on "Minor's Holiday" Ken hanging on
to Anitra's theme as if some folksinger
hopped a freight & swung by its ladder
with rails clicked him to a distant town

after he'd watched the V-shaped flocks
honking high overhead as the Sunshine
Special blew lonesome 'cross its tracks
he'd find a *Bull Durham* roll-your-own

that tramp's butt he'd smoke on the sly
since at home no tobacco no one drank
only watermelon under a star-filled sky
as bullfrogs sang to an ice cream crank

soaking up & absorbing nature's music
began with the rooster's morning crow
from their mud hole the grunt of a sow
with nightfall growls croaks & crickets

in spring a mateless mocker urging on
the one out there with a singing meant
for her alone outlined by a risen moon
his lyricsless call "This Is the Moment"

in '58 K's rendition of Robin's words
in the same year his "Where Are You"
from that team of Adamson-McHugh
but had known their songs from birds

living six miles out had rarely bought
Fairfield paper as vagabonds brought
earlier news of Rangers busting a still
remembered chasing of a Villa or Dill-

inger a Baby Face or read special bul-
letins on the poem of Bonnie & Clyde
written in her blood before she'd died
of 10 G-men dead in Big D gun battle

knew a nearer death in old board well
from when a curious cat had fallen in
as the bucket rose so would the smell
with their water rotten dug a new one

knew too the windmill's metal clang
lifted precious liquid from far below
with curved fan blades turning sang
a pumping song made the cattle low

knew the ubiquitous plains machine
with self-governed centrifugal force
saved in drought cow sheep & horse
kept okra beans & other truck green

Go-devil or Mock if it wasn't theirs
was a "weathered gray-wood affair"
served him to write & title his tune
on Blue Note's *Whistle Stop* of '61

to Ira Gitler his tonal talk's romantic
but the tempo's far too fast & frantic
Philly Joe's skins so thunder & thud
it goes against setting a tender mood

maybe waited for her in shadows cast
by nighttime's one-eyed ogling moon
but "Sunset" with Hank Mobley's sax
sounds more evocative of rendezvous

with racism blatantly raising its head
in the street & anywhere would trade
were kept in their place labeled shift-
less said rotgut & dice their only drift

to this Kenny perhaps a bit oblivious
for luckily able to sell all his buckets
of beans okra tomatoes & fresh juicy
plums to Watt Parker owned the city

& as head of the telephone exchange
gave KD a penny to fetch any person
received a call its 3-short-1-long ring
he to answer even if not a Beethoven

in the 1890s on hauling corn by oxen
Watt letting horse & buggy pass him
but vowed one day he too would own
such a newfangled classy contraption

in later decades just two months after
the Market crash he'd open his dealer-
ship then have the gin & hospital built
better roads for selling his automobile

the banker-president of Fairfield State
chair of bond drive with world at war
attending '48 Convention as delegate
for Democrats & owned his 300-acre

plot with its weeds Ken had chopped
while his poppa handled for Mr. Watt
his four big young mules of top stock
& to drive his new International truck

delivering workers to the highway site
20 miles distant brought hardly wealth
but relief as two-lane neared the white
rented four-room house sat up on stilts

once living in one-room shotgun type
with along one side their rowboat tied
for spring when Trinity River to flood
cover feral animals & cattle with mud

panthers or bobcats killed the old cow
desperadoes in making their getaways
to ditch the stolen cars far out of town
in the land's lovely unending embrace

these the fragments he'd later jot down
rounding-ups led to his rhythmic drives
from calves cut out to notes like knives
not to carve but impart a sharper sound

delicious as Freestone County peaches
as stirring as Flash! Federal agents stop
interstate spree of cold-blooded thieves
satisfied in a way till he'd discover bop

with Bird & Cannonball ye-odle la-dee-
ing a cotton picker's very same melody
heard it on his dragging in his last sack
to weigh it & be paid a pittance of jack

with chases between a trumpet & tenor
non-violent exchanges with a rapid-fire
snare the alto bullets made none expire
but K's tones to slay boomed or tender

yet before they could to leave the farm
move to Austin take music by the horn
learn to go unthrown by buckaroo lines
bulldog etudes & scales in record times

Book Club Discussion Questions

1. Explain the meaning of the book's title and clarify your explanations by referring to "Denton" (p. 203) and "The Pilgrimage" (p. 231).

2. Discuss the character of Maria as revealed in the love poems that describe her through one or more activity or object associated with her (pp. 80, 140-152, and 211-225).

3. What ironies do you find in "Crawling Geese on the Texas Coast" (p. 33)?

4. How does the form of "A Wedding Sestina" help develop the main ideas of the poem (p. 86)?

5. Find two poems that contain something you consider humorous and explain what you find funny about each.

6. Explain in "Newgulf" (p. 177) how the son's music relates to the father's sulfur industry and the mother's life and death.

7. In what ways do the Nazca lines in Peru, which depict a leviathan, represent in the poem of that title the poetry of Nobel-Prize poet Pablo Neruda (p. 78).

8. Explain the contrast between points of view in "Before the Fire" (p. 121).

9. Consider the themes developed through artworks in "Petri in Texas, 1851-1857" (p. 153) and "Liberty Hill" (p. 185).

10. Discuss how in "O-Yo-De-Lay-Hee-Hoing" (p. 248) the Texas boyhood of the jazz trumpeter contributed to his career as a world-renowned musician.